Did You Know . . .

- The flamboyant life of Howard Hughes was the basis for Harold Robbins's scandalous bestseller *The Carpetbaggers*?

- The arrest and conviction of Dr. Sam Sheppard for the brutal slaying of his wife inspired the hit TV show and box-office smash *The Fugitive*?

- Nicole Kidman's dangerously manipulative femme fatale in *To Die For* was based on an actual murder case?

- The classic film *Sweet Smell of Success* found its cynical inspiration in the career of the ruthless and all-powerful columnist Walter Winchell?

DATE DUE

RIVERDALE
DATE DUE
04 15 04

DEMCO 128-8155

FOR REEL.

The Real-Life Stories That Inspired Some of the Most Popular Movies of All Time

HAROLD SCHECHTER & DAVID EVERITT

BERKLEY BOULEVARD BOOKS, NEW YORK

4. MOTION PICTURES
I. TITLE

FOR REEL

A Berkley Boulevard Book / published by arrangement with the authors

PRINTING HISTORY
Berkley Boulevard trade paperback edition / January 2000

The Penguin Putnam Inc. World Wide Web site address is
http://www.penguinputnam.com

ISBN: 0-425-17271-6

BERKLEY BOULEVARD
Berkley Boulevard Books are published by The Berkley Publishing Group,
a division of Penguin Putnam Inc.,
375 Hudson Street, New York, New York 10014.
BERKLEY BOULEVARD and its logo
are trademarks belonging to Penguin Putnam Inc.

Contents

Introduction

They call it the "Dream Factory" for a good reason. For nearly a century, Hollywood has been manufacturing fantasies for the masses—an endless supply of sensational stories, spectacular visions, electrifying thrills, and sweeping romantic adventures. From the daredevil exploits of the *Indiana Jones* trilogy to the gut-wrenching drama of *Jaws* to the hair-raising horrors of *Psycho* movies provide us with magical, larger-than-life experiences that couldn't possibly be found in everyday life.

Or could they?

Watching films like *Raiders of the Lost Ark*, *Jaws*, and *Psycho*, we are meant to be dazzled—wonderstruck—*amazed*. But the most amazing thing of all about these movies may be this: incredible as it seems, they were all based on real life!

"Indy" Jones may seem like the ultimate fantasy hero—a little boy's wish-fulfillment figure—yet there was a real, nineteenth-century archaeologist/adventurer named Giovanni Belzoni who may well have served as Indy's model. Quint, the monomaniacal charter-boat captain of *Jaws*, might appear to be a pure pop fabrication—a cartoon Captain Ahab—but he was actually inspired by a legendary shark hunter who still operates a fishing boat on Long Island. And *Psycho*'s schizoid Norman Bates (along with Buffalo Bill of *The Silence of the Lambs* and Leatherface of *The Texas Chainsaw Massacre*) was a fictional—and comparatively tame—rendition of a far scarier, true-life prototype: the notorious midwestern ghoul Ed Gein.

These are just a few of the eye-opening facts you'll find in the following pages, which reveal the true, documented stories behind some of the most memorable (and seemingly fantastical) films ever made.

Most moviegoers are completely unaware that some of the wildest flights of cinematic fantasy are firmly rooted in fact. But there's nothing new about this phenomenon. Filmmakers have been turning truth into fiction for decades, from Fritz Lang's 1931 thriller, *M*, to Steven Spielberg's World War II saga, *Saving Private Ryan*. Why are moviemakers—those masters of make-believe—drawn so irresistibly to reality? For one thing, making a film based on actual events gives them a chance to "improve" on life—to make it tidier, more romantic, or morally satisfying. A seamy, early twentieth-century con game, for example—run by a pair of unsavory real-life crooks—became a delightfully intricate scheme in *The Sting*, starring Paul Newman and Robert Redford as two of the most bighearted, charmingly attractive rogues ever to appear on screen.

At other times—most famously in *Citizen Kane*—moviemakers have used the cover of fiction as a way to attack real-life public figures without getting sued for libel (though, as readers will learn, Kane's flesh-and-blood prototype, newspaper magnate William Randolph Hearst, did not exactly take Orson Welles's thinly disguised biopic lying down).

Most often, though, the answer is contained in the old saw that "truth is stranger fiction." In its search for stories that will thrill, chill, enchant, and amaze audiences, Hollywood has often looked to the most wondrous source of all—real life. What screenwriter could have dreamed up the idea of a mild-mannered psychokiller who dresses like his dead mother? Or a dashing, globe-trotting archaeologist adept at raiding ancient tombs? Or an elegant young con artist who beguiles his victims by pretending to be Sidney Poitier's son? As the saying goes—you can't make stuff like that up.

As readers of our book will discover, moviemakers have often seized upon astounding, real-life stories of crime, horror, and adventure as the raw material for their most spectacular visions. But some films have also tapped into real life for more down-to-earth, though no less intriguing stories—for classic excursions into the realms of romance, politics, and showbiz itself. The bickering old comedians of *The Sunshine Boys*, for example, were inspired by Smith and Dale, one of the most popular acts of the vaudeville stage. The cagey, charismatic hero of *The Last Hurrah*, portrayed by Spencer Tracy, was patterned after Mayor James Curley of Boston (a politician of such amazing appeal that he once got elected to office while serving time in prison). Tom Cruise's romantic protagonist in *Jerry Maguire* was modelled after true-life sports agent Gary Wichard.

Of course, there are times when learning the truth behind an illusion can detract from the experience. Few things in life are more disappointing than the mundane explanation of a magic trick—the dreary realization that the world-famous miracle worker is nothing more than a cunning manipulator of mirrors, trapdoors, and wires. When Dorothy and her pals pull back the curtain and expose the Great Wizard as a blustering con man, their deep sense of betrayal is plainly written on their faces.

But that kind of disillusionment doesn't apply here. If anything, the excitement and wonder inspired by certain films are actually increased by the knowledge of their real-life sources. Knowing that *The Exorcist*, for example, was based on an actual, 1940s case of alleged demonic possession doesn't make the film any less gripping. On the contrary, it *adds* something to the film—a believe-it-or-not dimension that makes our experience of it that much more intense.

From the very inception of film, Hollywood has redesigned reality for us, turning true-life stories into vehicles of excitement, emotion, and wonder. And as you're about to discover, the actual stories behind these classic films are often just as fascinating as the fictionalized versions that end up on screen. Here, then, are the fifty most dramatic tales that have traveled from real to reel—from the unembellished pages of history books and newspapers to the shining cinematic world of (not quite) make-believe.

All the King's Men

When this Oscar-winning film was released in 1949, its story was already well known. The tale had won a Pulitzer Prize just three years earlier in its original incarnation as a novel by Robert Penn Warren. The public was also aware of the story's factual basis. It was this knowledge that played a role in making both the book and the film a success. The events depicted in the story were so extraordinary that they would have otherwise seemed improbable.

No other episode from American history has taught a more chilling lesson on the abuse of power than the career of Huey Long. No other American leader has imposed a more tyrannical regime than he did, first as governor then as senator of Louisiana, from 1928 to 1935. Robert Penn Warren taught at Louisiana State University while this so-called homegrown fascist was at the height of his power. The author published his fictionalized treatment of Long's rise and fall just eleven years after the political strongman's assassination, when his exploits were still relatively fresh in people's minds.

Viewers watching the film adaptation today are sure to be impressed by Robert Rossen's exceptional scripting and direction, and by Broderick Crawford's Oscar-winning performance as Willie Stark, an obscure country lawyer who goes on to seize control of the state government through demagoguery, intimidation, and corruption. But to truly appreciate the movie, it helps to become as familiar with the *real* Willie Stark, as viewers were in 1949.

Huey Long was born into a northern Louisiana farm family in 1893. Clearly determined as a young man to leave the farm behind, he set his sights on becoming a lawyer, even though his family lacked the funds for his higher education. He postponed his entrance into college in order to earn money as a traveling salesman, then went on to study in his spare time until, by the age of twenty-two, he passed his bar exam. Within three years he won his first election, securing the office of state railroad commissioner.

From his family, Long inherited a populist bent that championed Louisiana's poor against the privileges of the rich. He quickly put this perspective to work first as railroad commissioner then as public service commissioner. He fought successfully to keep telephone and railway rates within reach for lower-income people and attempted to raise taxes for the Standard Oil Company, one of the state's corporate giants that Long would continue to demonize throughout his career.

Long failed in his first campaign to become governor in 1924, but succeeded four years later. A fiery, outlandish orator, he tapped into the resentments of rural voters and railed against the wealthy elite. In office, he backed up his rhetoric with some dramatic reforms. As the Great Depression took hold, he put many unemployed people to work on a huge program of highway building and bridge construction. Even one of Long's severest critics had to admit that the new governor "took Louisiana out of the mud." Long also devoted himself to bettering education for his citizens. He pushed a bill through the legislature that authorized the distribution of free schoolbooks. He established night schools to teach reading and writing to the illiterate. He funded improvements at Louisiana State University. As Long produced results, the loyalty of his followers intensified. At a time of economic desperation, few of them seemed to care very much that the colorful Long, or "Kingfish," as he was called, was resorting to unscrupulous methods. Others, though, were becoming alarmed.

To get his bills passed, Long would offer state jobs in exchange for legislators' votes. He was also known to use state funds for his own personal purposes. In a particularly ominous move, he established a state police force entitled the Bureau of Criminal Identification, which quickly became his own private militia, a Louisianan breed of storm troopers, or "Huey's Cossacks," as they were known.

In 1932, the Kingfish moved on to Washington, D.C., as a Democratic U.S. senator. He strutted across the national political stage with an impractical "Share the Wealth" proposal and attracted even more attention by breaking with President Franklin Roosevelt, whom he considered insufficiently radical. Being a senator, though, did not mean that he had relinquished any local control in Louisiana. Through his puppet successor as governor, he still pulled the strings in the state capital of Baton Rouge. As prodigious as his authority was, he was not satisfied and soon embarked on a renewed quest for power.

For years, Long's enemies had thought of him as a virtual dictator. By the end of 1934, the adjective "virtual" became unnecessary. Personally patrolling the legislative chambers to keep his majority in line, he pushed through a package of bills designed to transfer all local authority to his errand boys in the state government. In one particularly frantic five-day session, he saw forty-four of his bills passed. He gained control of the Louisiana National Guard and all local police and fire departments. The state attorney general became the direct supervisor of all local district attorneys. The state assumed control over hirings and firings at all local school districts, restricted the power of local courts to supervise elections, and levied new taxes on large-circulation newspapers (especially if they had the audacity to criticize the Kingfish and his regime). The financial devastation and political turmoil of the 1930s spawned an age of tyrants around the world—Mussolini, Stalin, Hitler, Chiang, Franco. Long became the closest thing to an American equivalent.

His tenure as an American political strongman did not last long. One dirty trick too many led to his end. The final scenes of *All the King's Men* followed the real events quite closely.

In September of 1935, Long was targeting a political opponent by the name of B. Henry Pavy, a district judge from an influential family. Long attacked the judge on two fronts. He proposed a gerrymander bill that would engineer Pavy's defeat at his next election, and he also resorted to blackmail. In the film, Willie Stark threatens to unearth details of an unsavory business deal from an opposing judge's past. The judge commits suicide, and an outraged nephew guns Stark down. In real life, Huey Long, through his henchmen, threatened to revive an old forgotten rumor that there was African blood in the family of Judge Pavy's wife. In the days of the Jim Crow south, this was an incendiary charge. No suicide was needed to provoke one of the judge's family members. His son-in-law, a respected surgeon named Dr. Carl Austin Weiss, found Long in the capitol building, as would his fictional counterpart in the film. Both Weiss and Long were wounded in the exchange of gunfire between assassin and bodyguards. Weiss died instantly. Louisiana's homespun dictator expired two days later.

Badlands

"**Thrill-Hungry Teens on** a Reckless Rampage!" . . . "They Live, Love and Even Kill for Kicks!" . . . "Savage Punks on a Binge of Violence!" Ad lines like these screamed from posters for a slew of B movies from the fifties and sixties. Strutting through these melodramas were black-jacketed, DA'ed young hoods and gum-chomping, loose-living teenage girls. In such lurid flicks as *Dragstrip Riot*, *Wild Youth*, and *The Cool and the Crazy*, teen heavies drove fast, sneered at every conceivable family value, and nurtured a frightening penchant for senseless brutality.

Clearly, movies of this kind represented the worst fears of every Eisenhower-era parent. It wasn't just that the films themselves were unsettling. The facts *behind* the movies were what really disturbed people. Street-gang rumbles and random teen mayhem repeatedly made headlines at the time, prompting civic groups and congressional committees to question the direction taken by American youth. One story of teenage nihilism, though, loomed above all others, revolving around two wayward youths who embodied this new criminal trend more than any other—the Nebraskan greaser named Charlie Starkweather and his teenybopper accomplice, Caril Ann Fugate. Their 1958 murder spree indirectly fueled any number of low-budget potboilers. More clearly and more directly it inspired the 1973 sleeper *Badlands*, the first film by maverick director Terrence Malick, and one of the most chilling crime films ever made.

A young Martin Sheen and Cissy Spacek costarred, respectively, as the protagonists Kit Carruthers and Holly Sargis. Although the names and some of the facts were changed, there could be no doubt that the source of the film was the Starkweather/Fugate rampage that spread terror across the American heartland and left ten people dead in just nine days.

The true story behind *Badlands* began in Lincoln, Nebraska, during the winter of 1957. Charlie Starkweather, age nineteen, was a short, bowlegged punk who slicked back his hair and smoked cigarettes out of the corner of his mouth in the manner of celluloid rebel James Dean. Until then his accomplishments in life consisted of dropping out of school during the ninth grade and getting fired from his job as a garbageman. Lack of employment left him time to pursue what was really important to him: hot rods, guns, and underage girls. His sweetheart at the time was fourteen-year-old Caril Ann Fugate, who hung around with the reprobate Starkweather despite the objections of her mother and stepfather.

On December 1, 1957, Starkweather rehearsed for the exploits that would soon make him a tabloid headliner. Armed with a shotgun, he held up a gas station on the outskirts of the city. The only one there was a twenty-one-year-old attendant named Robert Colvert. He didn't make any trouble for the young stickup man. Still, Starkweather felt it necessary to abduct the attendant, take him out into the country, and blow his brains out. For the next seven weeks, Starkweather managed not to murder anyone else. Then, on January 21, 1958, he began his desperado career in earnest.

On that day Starkweather showed up at Caril Fugate's small lower-class home and waited for her to return from school. Her parents were not pleased with the presence of the glowering young man. There was tension in the air. Tension was not something Charlie Starkweather dealt with especially well. He took umbrage at something that was said and shot both Caril's mother and stepfather with his .22 slide-action hunting rifle. Starkweather then pummeled his girlfriend's two-year-old half sister with his rifle butt and slit her throat. Around this time, Caril Ann Fugate returned home.

How much of all this slaughter Fugate actually witnessed has never been clear. She later claimed that Charlie hid the bodies before she had the chance to discover what had happened. On the other hand, the single-story house was so small that it would have been difficult to conceal a triple murder from someone else occupying the same cramped quarters. Whatever Fugate did or did not know, she certainly did not act like someone terribly concerned about her missing family. Shortly after the murders, she was cuddling on the couch with Starkweather, eating sandwiches and watching TV. She stayed in the house with him for the next six days. For his part, Starkweather viewed all this in romantic terms—or, at least, his idea of romantic terms. As he later put it: "We knowed that the world had give us to each other. We was goin' to make it leave us alone." He put a sign on the front door: STAY A WAY. EVERY BODY IS SICK WITH THE FLU.

When Fugate's relatives began to get suspicious, the teen lovers took off in Starkweather's souped-up '49 Ford. They moved very quickly over the next two days. On a farm southeast of the city, Starkweather killed a seventy-year-old man, then kidnapped and murdered a high-school couple. He raped the girl before shooting her. Traveling back to Lincoln, with Fugate still at his side, he broke into a wealthy home where he stabbed to death Clara Ward and her maid, then fatally shot Mrs. Ward's husband.

Panic seized the area. The local sheriff formed a hundred-man posse, the state governor called out the National Guard, parents kept children home from school, and companies booked hotels for their employees so that they would not have to travel home on roads where the killer couple might be roaming. But the alarm would not last long. The same day that the bodies were discovered in the Ward home, police in Colorado ran the fugitives down. Starkweather had just shot a traveling salesman nine times in order to acquire his car.

At his trial, Starkweather actually considered arguing self-defense, until his lawyer convinced him to try an insanity plea instead. Crazy as Charlie obviously was, this approach did not work. He died in the electric chair on June 25, 1958. As for Caril Ann Fugate, she claimed she had not been an accomplice but had been Starkweather's hostage during the entire nine-day spree. This tack did not work either. She was sentenced to life in prison. Eighteen years later, though, she succeeded in winning parole. At the time, she told reporters, "I just want to be an ordinary dumpy little housewife—wash the socks, burn the toast."

Five years after Starkweather's execution, the first fictionalized film version of the case appeared. Low-budget, grimy, and intense, *The Sadist* starred Arch Hall Jr. as a teen psycho who holds three teachers hostage. The stark black-and-white camera work came courtesy of future Oscar-winning cinematographer Vilmos Zsigmond. There was also an official docudrama of the case in 1993, the TV film *Murder in the Heartland*, featuring Tim Roth and Fairuza Balk as Starkweather and Fugate. Although it follows the facts closely, the movie fails in one very important department: it is altogether too coy and noncommittal about the extent of Fugate's involvement in the murders.

Badlands, on the other hand, presents a very clear interpretation of the role played by the fictional Holly Sargis, the killer's girlfriend. Not that she plays an active part in the murders. Rather, she is alarmingly passive. As emotionally stunted as her lover Kit (whose killings seem more careless than ferocious), she blithely accompanies her boyfriend on his corpse-strewn trail, as if she were merely hitching a ride to the local malt shop. In the end, the only lesson she learns is that it is perhaps best not to hang around with "the hell-bent type."

Barton Fink

John Turturro stars as the eponymous hero in this bizarro 1991 comedy by the inimitable Coen brothers. Wearing thick-framed black eyeglasses and an *Eraserhead* hairdo, Barton is a cartoon carica- ture of a New York Jewish intellectual circa 1940. The first scene of the movie takes place on opening night of Barton's socially conscious Broadway play, *Bare Ruined Choirs*, a painfully earnest drama about fishmongers that is meant to celebrate the "triumph of the Common Man."

When his play receives a rave review in the *Herald* ("The playwright finds nobility in the most squalid quarters and poetry in the most cal- lous speech"), the utterly humorless, hopelessly self-important Barton is immediately offered a Hollywood contract that his agent finds hard to refuse. Heading off to la-la land with his Underwood portable and pretentious dreams of creating a new kind of drama that will help "ease the suffering of one's fellowman," Barton is given the job of writing a Wallace Beery wrestling picture. Trapped in the world's creepiest hotel room, he finds himself suffering from the worst case of writer's block since the one that afflicted Jack Nicholson in *The Shining*. To make matters worse, his next-door neighbor, an affable lug played by John Goodman, turns out to be a serial killer from hell (literally).

Combining hilarious Hollywood satire with horror-movie excess, *Barton Fink* is a pure unadulterated product of the Coen brothers' febrile imaginations. Two of its major characters, however, are modeled on real-life people. One of Barton's fellow contract writers—an urbane southern lush named William P. Mayhew, who, in the film, is considered America's greatest living novelist—is a comical version of Nobel Prize–winning author William Faulkner, who did a stint in Hollywood. And Fink himself is modeled on a writer who has largely been forgotten but who, at one time, was regarded as the country's preeminent young playwright, Clifford Odets.

Born in Philadelphia in 1906, Odets was the only son of Jewish immigrant parents. His father, Louis, was a printer by trade. In 1912, the family moved to the Bronx, where—during a first-grade production of *Cinderella* (in which he was cast as Prince Charming)—the six-year-old boy was bitten by the acting bug and resolved to make the theater his life.

Though Odets passed his early years in modest circumstances, his go-getter father moved steadily up the economic ladder, eventually becoming the owner of a printing plant. Before long, the family had achieved significant prosperity and was enjoying the fruits of pre–World War I, upper-middle-class success: a handsome apartment, a fancy automobile, a phonograph.

Though a voracious reader, Odets was always an indifferent student and spent much of his teen years at the movies or immersed in books. He was a particular fan of French novelist Victor Hugo (author of *Les Misérables*) and daydreamed about becoming a champion of the downtrodden and outcast. In high school, he distinguished himself in school plays and oratory contests but did so poorly in the classroom that he dropped out after his sophomore year.

For the next six years, he acted with various amateur groups, made a paltry income as a radio announcer and drama critic, worked in vaudeville, and held a succession of humdrum jobs (bookkeeper, Fuller Brush salesman, etc.). In 1929, Louis Odets sold his business for a small fortune and returned to Philadelphia, settling into a big house in a fashionable neighborhood. Twenty-three-year-old Clifford, still a struggling, virtually penniless actor and playwright, moved back in with his parents and joined a local drama company. He also wrote a number of radio plays, one of which aired on stations in both New York City and Philadelphia.

In 1929, Odets returned to New York City to understudy Spencer Tracy in the Broadway play *Conflict*. Though the play flopped, Odets remained in Manhattan, where, over the next few years, he played small parts in various productions.

By then, the Great Depression was under way. Solitary and dejected, the struggling young actor and playwright empathized with the plight of those whose lives had been devastated by the social upheaval of the time. He still aspired to be a champion of the dispossessed (like his literary hero, Victor Hugo) and to use his pen to combat the suffering he saw all around him.

The turning point in his life (and career) came in 1931 when he joined the Group Theater, an organization dedicated to staging socially conscious works. In 1935, Odets's short but deeply rousing protest play *Waiting for Lefty* became an instant sensation. Informed by the author's political sympathies, this crude but effective play takes the form of a labor union meeting. As a group of taxi drivers debates a proposed strike on stage, actors planted in the audience arise from their seats to shout out their feelings. The play ends with the news that the union leader, "Lefty" Costello, has been found murdered, a disclosure that leads to the climactic rallying cry to action:

> *Hear it, boys, hear it? Hell, listen to me! Coast to coast! HELLO AMERICA! HELLO. WE'RE STORMBIRDS OF THE WORKING-CLASS. WORKERS OF THE WORLD . . . OUR BONES AND BLOOD! And when we die they'll know what we did to make a new world! Christ, cut us up to little pieces. We'll die for what is right! Put fruit trees where our ashes are!*

The opening scene of *Barton Fink* is meant to evoke the triumphant premiere of *Waiting for Lefty*, and the idealistic playwright portrayed by John Turturro is a satiric version of the youthful Odets. What happened in real life bears little resemblance to the surreal misadventures that befall the Coens' hapless hero, except in one major respect. Like Barton Fink, Odets was unable to resist a hugely lucrative offer to write for the movies. By the early 1940s, he was residing largely in Hollywood, and his life (and art) would never be the same.

Though he continued to write sporadically for the theater, the bulk of Odets's work for the rest of his life consisted of screenplays and television scripts. Constantly derided for "selling out" to Hollywood, he himself was deeply conflicted over the direction his career had taken. On occasion, he would stoutly defend his work, insisting that movie writing had taught him invaluable lessons about dramatic construction. At other times, however, he seemed filled with self-hatred, bitterly describing himself as a "playwright manqué," who had peddled his artistic gifts for mere material comfort. In the late 1940s, an interviewer asked him, "Suppose there was no film industry today. Where would you be?"

"Well, in some ways it would have been better for me," Odets replied, "because I might have been more productive in the serious aspects of my work instead of the mere craft aspects. I would have scrounged this way and that . . . and good would have come out of it, more good than has come out of my present way of life."

Odets's bitterness toward the richly paid but artistically sterile way of life he had chosen was most fully expressed in his 1949 play, *The Big Knife*, about an idealistic actor who sells out to the movies and ends up leading a life of such hollowness and hypocrisy that he finally commits suicide. Though Odets continued to live on in comfort until his death from stomach cancer in 1963, many critics felt that he, too, had committed artistic suicide by going out to Hollywood—an assessment that seems confirmed by the arc of a career which began with the Broadway triumph of *Waiting for Lefty* and ended with the screenplay for the 1961 Elvis Presley vehicle, *Wild in the Country*.

The Bridge on the River Kwai

Movies—**particularly great** ones—pack so much imaginative power that their version of reality can easily supplant historical truth. In their so-called battle over *Citizen Kane*, media czar William Randolph Hearst might have dealt a fatal blow to Orson Welles's career. But it was Welles who had the last laugh, making it impossible to think about Hearst without immediately picturing Charles Foster Kane—the lonely, embittered recluse, abandoned by everyone who ever cared about him. And when people think of Count Laszlo Almasy, the hero of the romantic epic *The English Patient*, they will forever conjure up the image of dashing Ralph Fiennes and not the hollow-chested, homosexual Nazi spy that the fictional character was based on (and named after).

Aware of this phenomenon, the man whose grueling World War II experiences became the basis of *The Bridge on the River Kwai* made an effort to set the record straight before he died. Understandably enough, he did not want David Lean's cinematic epic to stand as the definitive version of the story. And he himself did not wish to be remembered in light of Alec Guinness's Colonel Nicholson, an officer whose unyielding obstinacy, pride, and perfectionism lead him to commit something very close to collaboration. In reality, the British commander whose men helped construct the infamous Kwai bridge was a far more admirable, even heroic, figure than the stiff-necked military fanatic portrayed in the movie.

The real-life "man behind the bridge" was Lieutenant Colonel Philip Toosey. Born in Birkenhead, England, in 1904, he worked as a banker and cotton trader in Liverpool before World War II broke out. In 1941, he was posted to Singapore, where he took part in the sixteen-day siege that culminated in the surrender of the British garrison on February 15, 1942—the single worst defeat in British military history. One of the few commanders to distinguish himself during the battle, Toosey (who was awarded a Distinguished Service medal for his conduct) was ordered to evacuate the city before it fell. However, he refused to abandon his men. As a result, he became one of the 130,000 Allied soldiers taken prisoner by the Japanese.

In 1942, in preparation for an invasion of India, the Japanese army decided to build a railway connection between Thailand and Burma, through 258 miles of dense, mountainous jungle. Once this link was completed, the army would be able to move troops and three thousand tons of supplies each day from Bangkok to Rangoon. The plan called for the use of Allied POWs as the primary workforce.

In October 1942, Toosey and 650 men from various regiments were shipped in overcrowded, underventilated freight cars to the Tamarkan POW camp in Burma, where they were ordered to build two bridges—one of steel, one of wood—over the Kwai River. In the movie, there is only one bridge, and its design and construction are almost entirely the result of British know-how and enterprise. The Japanese having bungled the project, Colonel Nicholson takes charge and sets out to build the best bridge possible, as a way of both maintaining the morale of his men and proving the superiority of the English. Before long, the bridge becomes his pride and joy; indeed, he has more invested in its successful completion than the Japanese. By the time the film is over, he has so completely lost perspective that—when a team of Allied commandos shows up to dynamite the bridge—Nicholson betrays his own side rather than see his precious monument destroyed (though, in a final moment of either heroism or ironic accident, he himself blows up the bridge when he falls dead across the plunger).

All of this bears only the most tenuous relationship to the truth. For one thing, the notion that the Japanese were too incompetent to design a railway bridge in the jungle was (as Toosey himself told an interviewer) "absolute rubbish." The Kwai bridges were not only marvels of engineering but were completed in record time. Toosey and his men supplied nothing but raw manpower to supplement the Japanese workforce.

It is true that—in violation of the Geneva Convention (which prohibited POWs from doing any work that was useful to the enemy)—Toosey cooperated with his captors by ordering his men to work on the project. He was also a strict disciplinarian, who did not hesitate to mete out punishment to malingerers. But his motives had nothing to do with chauvinistic pride, let alone self-glorification. Rather, he did what was necessary to ensure the survival of his charges. He knew that if he refused to paricipate in the construction of the bridges, he and his men would be machine-gunned without hesitation.

Moreover, by cooperating with the Japanese, he was able to win important benefits for his men—extra rations and medical supplies, a certain amount of rest and recreation. Even so (and in contrast to the fictional Colonel Nicholson, who forbids any act of sabotage), Toosey and fellow POWs did whatever they could to undermine the project by mixing defective cement and, at one point, infesting the timber with all the termites they could gather. Another major difference betwen Toosey and Nicholson was their attitude toward escape. Guinness's character refuses to allow his subordinates to form an escape committee. By contrast, when two of his officers attempted to flee the camp, Toosey supplied them with enough hard rations to last a month and waited forty-eight hours before reporting them missing. As punishment for the breakout, he was forced to stand at attention for twelve hours in the blazing tropical sun. Indeed, Toosey—who accepted full responsibility for his men and did his best to protect them—often bore the brunt of the enemy's displeasure and endured regular beatings.

If Toosey was a considerably more appealing figure than his cinematic counterpart, so was his real-life antagonist, whose name (as in the film) was Major Saito. In the movie, Saito (played by Sessue Hayakawa) is every bit as obstinate and fanatical as Nicholson—a ruthless martinet who lives by the Japanese code of Bushido and disdains the British as a bunch of pantywaists. The actual Saito was, by all accounts, one of the most reasonable and humane of the Japanese officers. He was open to negotiations with Toosey and willing to grant the prisoners concessions in return for their cooperation. By war's end, Toosey's respect for Saito was such that he spoke up on his behalf at the War Crimes Tribunal, saving him from the gallows.

The Kwai bridges were completed in May 1943, just seven months after construction began. In the thrilling climax of the movie, the bridge is blown up just as the first Japanese supply train is crossing it. In reality, the Kwai bridges were used for two years, making it possible for the Japanese to transport enormous quantities of ammunition, food, supplies, and troops to Burma. On June 24, 1945, they were finally destroyed by an RAF squadron, which demolished three spans of the metal bridge and completely obliterated the wooden one.

By then, Toosey had been transferred to another POW camp. Altogether, he remained in captivity for three and a half years. At the end of the war, he returned to Liverpool, resumed his banking career, and—in his very British, stiff-upper-lip way—rarely spoke about his war experiences. Even after the release of *The Bridge on the River Kwai* in 1957, he refused to comment publicly about its inaccuracies, in spite of repeated requests from fellow veterans. Ultimately, however, he was persuaded to talk by a British history professor named Peter Davies. Together they taped forty-eight hours of interviews which formed the basis of Davies's 1991 book, *The Man Behind the Bridge*.

Toosey died in 1975. It is a testimony to Saito's character that, ten years later, he made a pilgrimage to England to pay a visit to Philip Toosey's grave.

The Carpetbaggers

Few public figures have attracted as much lurid attention as Howard Hughes. Between his string of affairs with Hollywood starlets, his daring aviation feats, and his descent into madness, the tycoon's tumultuous life was a tabloid editor's dream come true. It was also, inevitably, grist for the seamy-bestseller mill. The book that this mill eventually produced turned out to be the perfect match of subject and author—America's most outlandish magnate and the country's most irresistibly sleazy novelist.

The Carpetbaggers, published in 1961, was one of Harold Robbins's early commercial successes, a definitive example of his page-turning mix of power, money, and sex. The 1964 film version may have toned down the book's more sensational elements—it steered clear, for instance, of such things as the incestuous affair between siblings and the bloody Indian prenuptial ritual—but, for what it's worth, the movie captured the garish, low-down appeal of Harold Robbins better than any other "filmization." The movie revolves around a Hughes-like tycoon named Jonas Cord (played with icy, arrogant panache by George Peppard) who parlays his father's fortune and his own ruthless business savvy into a smarmy sideline as a Hollywood mogul. When it comes to guilty pleasures, few movies offer such unabashed, trashy entertainment. And both Robbins and the filmmakers owe it all, ultimately, to the enigmatic man who fashioned the real-life template for these sordid escapades.

The movie's opening scenes are filled with similarities between fact and fiction. Like Hughes, Jonas Cord Jr. is named after his successful father and inherits the family business as a young man when his father suddenly dies. Acting shrewdly beyond his years, as Hughes himself did, he assumes total control by quickly buying out the other stockholders. Cord's interest in airplanes then leads him to acquire an airline company, and before long he revolutionizes the passenger air-travel industry (the name of Cord's company is International Airways, a paraphrase of Hughes's Trans World Airlines).

Most of the movie concerns Cord's involvement in Hollywood, corresponding to one of the most intriguing and salacious chapters in Hughes's career. Cord is drawn into the movie industry through a set of unusual circumstances. His friend Nevada Smith, a former western outlaw turned cowboy star, needs an influx of money to save his latest production. Cord agrees to bail him out. Hughes, however, did not need circumstance to lead him into the film business. From an early age, he was fascinated by movies and was determined to become the industry's greatest producer.

His first film most definitely did not earn him that distinction. A 1926 sentimental drama entitled *Swell Hogan*, it was such a dog that distributors refrained from unleashing it on the unsuspecting public. To make sure that his next ventures wouldn't duplicate this disaster, Hughes proceeded to school himself in the filmmaking process, visiting movie sets, watching professionals at work, filling twenty notebooks with his observations. The homework paid off: his next two productions made profits. From there he plunged into the movie that would make his reputation as a brilliant, extravagant, and obsessive filmmaker.

Hell's Angels, an aerial World War I saga, was the most expensive movie ever made at the time of its release, costing $4 million in an era when the average film was brought in for $150,000. Much of the budget went into procuring Hughes's own little air force of forty fighter planes to be featured in the spectacular air warfare scenes. Another chunk of the budget was spent simply on waiting. On some days, the planes and the high-priced pilots remained idle on the ground for hours until the clouds overhead clustered picturesquely enough for Hughes to commence filming. Most critics agreed that the time and money spent on these scenes were worth it—the aerial combat sequences were extraordinary. However, in the process of filming the airborne stunts, three pilots died. Producer-director Hughes came close to becoming fatality number four. Against the advice of his more experienced airmen, he performed an especially reckless flight stunt himself and ended up diving out of control and crashing at high speed into the runway. Somehow he survived, but he sustained head injuries that may have exacerbated his already erratic mental condition.

In 1929, after working on the movie for nearly two years, Hughes raised the budget even higher when he decided to convert his silent epic into a talkie. This meant reshooting many of the scenes. It also meant recasting the leading lady. The part of the English temptress had been played by a Scandinavian actress named Greta Nissen, whose accent now disqualified her for the role. To replace her, Hughes signed up an unknown bit player named Jean Harlow. Her conspicuously American accent was not particularly suited to the part either, but the voluptuous starlet added a sexual charge to the film that was daring for its time. Hughes had a brief affair with Harlow, the first of many sexual adventures with a staggering array of beautiful stars that would include Katharine Hepburn, Rita Hayworth, Yvonne De Carlo, Cyd Charisse, and Lana Turner.

In *The Carpetbaggers*, the Nevada Smith movie produced by Jonas Cord is actually a fictional composite of Hughes's two most famous films, *Hell's Angels* and *The Outlaw*. Like *Hell's Angels*, the Cord production is converted to sound and features a Harlow-like blond bombshell (named Rina Marlowe and played by Carroll Baker, who would go on a year later to portray the legendary actress officially in *Harlow*). Like *The Outlaw*, the Cord film is designed to bring sex to westerns.

It was in *The Outlaw*, of course, that Hughes cast the busty Jane Russell and designed a special bra to show off her endowments without revealing any telltale outline of an undergarment beneath her blouse. Actually, unbeknownst to Hughes, Russell refused to wear the specially engineered contraption. Instead, she contrived the desired smooth look by inserting tissues into the top of her normal bra. Hughes, who was beginning to grow more unstable, spent hours filming take after take of his starlet to capture her cleavage on film exactly as he thought it should be. Ten years later, when he was head of RKO, Hughes pursued this obsession even further. Producing another Russell film entitled *Macao*, he drafted a four-page memo devoted entirely to the actress's breasts and how they should be photographed.

By the time Hughes left the movie business in 1955, his mind was already beginning to unravel. He had turned into a recluse and had become so fearful of germs that he would only touch objects if his hand was covered with Kleenex. By the 1970s, the disintegration was complete. Once a dashing pilot and womanizer, he was now reduced to an emaciated ninety-five pounds, his hair hanging well below his shoulders and his fingernails grown to Fu Manchu length.

At the end of *The Carpetbaggers*, we learn that Jonas Cord has been haunted by an overpowering fear. His twin brother had died while a child, a hopeless psychotic, and ever since Cord has feared that he, too, would plunge into madness. Ultimately, he realizes that he will escape this family curse. In reality, of course, Howard Hughes became, in effect, Jonas Cord's twin, rescued from an early death but doomed to hermitlike dementia.

Citizen Kane

"I anticipated trouble from Hearst for that reason."

—Orson Welles, referring to the highly unflattering portrait of Charles Kane's Marion Davies–like mistress, Susan

Ever since he was a little boy, Orson Welles had been told that he was a great creative genius—and by the time he reached his twenties, he seemed well on his way to fulfilling every extravagant expectation people had of him. In 1935, his so-called voodoo *Macbeth*—a revolutionary staging of Shakespeare's classic set in Haiti and featuring an all-black cast of Harlem actors—was the talk of New York City. Shortly afterward, he stunned theatergoers with a version of *Julius Caesar* that turned the play into a powerful allegory about the rise of modern fascism. He was only twenty-three years old when he was featured on the cover of *Time* magazine, which hailed him as "the brightest moon that has risen over Broadway in many years." Perhaps his greatest coup occurred on Halloween night, 1938, when, along with his Mercury Players, he broadcast a radio rendition of H. G. Wells's *War of the Worlds*. Millions of listeners, tuning in to the program (which took the form of realistically simulated news bulletins), believed that Martian invaders had landed in New Jersey and were obliterating everything in their path. The show set off a nationwide panic and made Welles a household name.

In 1939—at the age of only twenty-four—the "Boy Wonder of the American theater" headed west to conquer Hollywood. RKO studio rolled out the red carpet for him, offering him the kind of contract other filmmakers could only dream of: complete creative control of two motion pictures of his choosing. At first, Welles planned to do a version of Joseph Conrad's *Heart of Darkness*, but the project was eventually scrapped (Conrad's classic tale about a man who journeys deep into the savage jungle to find a power-mad renegade wouldn't make it to the big screen until 1979, when Francis Ford Coppola used it as the basis of his Vietnam epic, *Apocalypse Now*). Next, Welles considered filming a British thriller, *Smiler with a Knife*, but that project also fell through. For a while, it seemed as if his Hollywood experience might end in an unprecedented defeat for the wunderkind. And then, Welles's screenwriter pal, Herman Mankiewicz, proposed an idea that had been percolating in his head for a while—a cinematic saga based on the life of media magnate William Randolph Hearst. Welles immediately leaped at the notion.

Hearst was a figure of epic proportions. Born into enormous wealth (his father, George, had amassed one of the largest mining fortunes in the west), he had been raised by an adoring mother who instilled in him an inordinate sense of his own greatness and destiny. (During his first grand tour of Europe at the age of ten, he was deeply disappointed that his mother couldn't buy him the one souvenir he wanted most—the Louvre.)

After two notably undistinguished years at Harvard, he turned his attention to the newspaper business, taking control of the *San Francisco Examiner* (one of his father's many properties) and immediately boosting its circulation by filling it with sensational stories, lurid illustrations, and other features that made it appealing to the working masses. But San Francisco wasn't a big enough stage for Hearst's overweening ambition—or his colossal ego. In 1895, at the age of thirty-two, he moved to New York City to take on newspaper czar Joseph Pulitzer. Purchasing a failing paper, the *Morning Journal,* Hearst quickly turned it into the city's biggest-selling daily by stealing away the best writers on Pulitzer's staff and filling the *Journal*'s pages with lurid crime stories, blaring headlines, jingoistic sentiments, colored magazine inserts, and popular comic strips. Before long, he had become the most dominant newspaper publisher in the world, a man with the power not only to shape public opinion but to detemine the destiny of the whole nation. To a large extent, it was the *Journal*'s sensationalistic newspaper coverage of supposed Spanish atrocities in Cuba that led to the Spanish-American War. (According to one widely told story, when artist Frederic Remington was dispatched to Cuba to provide illustrations for Hearst's papers, he wired back that he couldn't find any war. "You furnish the pictures," Hearst heatedly replied. "I'll furnish the war.")

As the twentieth century got under way, Hearst began establishing newspapers in cities throughout the country—Boston, Chicago, Atlanta, Seattle, Los Angeles. By the early 1920s, one out of every five Americans read a Hearst paper. Eventually, his empire expanded to include every branch of the media—books, magazines, radio, motion pictures. With unprecedented control of the public's news and entertainment sources, he began to pursue his ultimate ambition—to preside, not just over the nation's media, but over the nation itself. But his repeated campaigns for high political office—mayor of New York City, governor of New York, U.S. president—all ended in failure. By the time the country entered World War I, his enemies mockingly referred to him as William Also-Randolph Hearst.

Still, there were consolations. On his "ranch" in the mountains north of Hollywood—an expanse of land half the size of Rhode Island—he built his princely estate, San Simeon. He stocked his castle with antiques, artworks, and monuments purchased from around the globe (at one point, Hearst alone accounted for an astonishing 25 percent of the world's art market). He installed the world's largest private zoo for the enjoyment of his guests. And he installed something—or rather, some*one*—else for his own enjoyment: his eighteen-year-old mistress, former chorus girl and self-avowed gold digger, Marion Davies.

A charming, vivacious beauty, Davies was a natural-born comedienne. Hearst, however—in an effort to turn her into the next Sarah Bernhardt—cast her in a series of elaborate vanity productions: stuffy, overblown costume dramas which (in spite of all his efforts) he was unable to shove down the public's throat. Davies quickly became a critical laughingstock. But she was genuinely devoted to Hearst. And with her great *joie de vivre* and Tinseltown friendships, she turned San Simeon into a gathering place for Hollywood's elite. Every Saturday night, Hearst and Marion hosted riotous costume parties, attended by some of the most glamorous stars and powerful men in the world. Hearst might have turned San Simeon into "the place God would have built, if He had the money" (as George Bernard Shaw described it), but it was Marion who filled it with gaiety and life.

By 1939, Hearst was a seventy-six-year-old man whose fortune had been seriously damaged by the Great Depression. But he was far from over-the-hill, and the killer instincts that had turned him into one of the most feared men in America hadn't diminished at all—as the twenty-four-year-old Welles would soon discover to his everlasting regret.

Though Mankiewicz and Welles made no bones about basing their main character on Hearst, there are important differences between the fictional Charles Foster Kane and his real-life counterpart. For one thing, their backgrounds are different—Hearst was born into enormous wealth, whereas Kane is the son of poor boardinghouse proprietors who accidentally come into a fortune and ship their son off to be raised as the ward of a bank executor named Bernstein. (Indeed, as various critics have noted, Kane's childhood is closer to that of Welles, who was orphaned at thirteen and placed in the care of a man named Bernstein.) Welles himself saw Kane as "better than Hearst"—more charming and likable, more genuinely idealistic (at least at first).

Still, from the opening sequence of the film—which shows Kane dying horribly alone in a Gothic mansion that seems more like the House of Usher than San Simeon—*Citizen Kane* offers a brutal depiction of its Hearst-like protagonist. In reality, Hearst was something of a party animal—a man with a tremendous gusto for and involvement with life. He was far from the stiff, embittered, isolated figure in Welles's film. Even so, it wasn't the scathing picture of himself that provoked Hearst's anger. As one of the most powerful men in America, he'd endured far nastier attacks throughout his life. What really enraged him was Welles's savage caricature of the woman he adored, Marion Davies, who is represented in the film by Kane's shrill, bubble-brained, utterly talentless mistress, Susan Alexander.

As soon as he learned about *Citizen Kane*, Hearst did everything possible to have it suppressed. He threatened to expose scandalous doings among studio executives and stars; to prohibit his papers from accepting movie advertisements; to launch a moral crusade against Hollywood. Terrified, Louis B. Mayer and other moguls banded together and tried to buy the negative of Welles's movie in order to destroy it. *Citizen Kane* became a *cause célèbre*. In the end, it was released to great critical acclaim. By the early 1960s, it was acknowledged as a masterpiece, and in 1998 was honored as the best American movie of all time.

Still, the controversy surrounding the movie cost Welles his career. By the time he was twenty-five, he was known as America's youngest has-been. He would never have total artistic control over another Hollywood film and would spend the rest of his days struggling to scrape together the funding to make his own films. Ironically, many modern critics have come to see *Citizen Kane* less as a story about William Randolph Hearst than as a grimly prescient fable about the brilliant rise and tragic decline of Welles himelf.

Dead Ringers

From the very start of his career—in films like *They Came from Within, Rabid,* and *Videodrome*—David Cronenberg has displayed a distinct queasiness about sex, the female anatomy, and the slimy, organic stuff that makes up the inside of our bodies. So it's no surprise that he was attracted to a project about a pair of brilliant (if wildly neurotic) twin gynecologists who are obsessed to the point of madness with the innermost secrets of the womb.

Released in 1988, *Dead Ringers* stars Jeremy Irons in a tour de force, dual performance. Thanks to brilliant special effects, Irons is able to play opposite himself as both Beverly and Eliot Mantle, identical twins so intensely bonded to each other that, by comparison, Chang and Eng seem like kissing cousins. Eliot—older than his brother by a few minutes—is a smooth-talking extrovert with a flair for speechmaking, fundraising, and seducing women by the score. Beverly is the studious, quiveringly sensitive type, who gets his occasional kicks by sleeping with his brother's hand-me-downs.

Though their relationship is intensely creepy—less symbiotic than incestuous—it seems to work for the Mantles, until their lives are turned upside down by Claire Niveau (Genevieve Bujold), a movie star whose unbeatable combination of traits—a taste for kinky sex and a "trifurcated uterus"—make her irresistibly alluring to the twins. After Eliot warms her up in bed, he passes her along to Bev, who (pretending to be Eliot) makes the dire mistake of falling in love with her. When Claire discovers that she has been shared by both brothers, she breaks up with Bev, who proceeds to drown his sorrows in sleeping pills and amphetamines. It isn't long before his twin also gets hooked. By the end of the film, the two have retreated into the womblike hell of their increasingly squalid condo, where they subsist on junk food and drugs. In a final, delirious attempt to sever the unholy tie that binds them, Bev performs a gruesome operation on his brother, disemboweling him with a nightmarish-looking gynecological implement. Bev, however, is unable to exist without his other half. The film's climactic shot shows their corpses intertwined amid the wreckage of their once elegant apartment.

When Cronenberg's movie was first released, few reviewers failed to note its striking resemblance to the story of the forty-five-year-old Marcus twins, Cyril and Stewart, internationally famous gynecologists who were found dead in their Manhattan luxury apartment in 1975. Though Cronenberg claimed that his movie had no relation to their case, his denial seems highly disingenuous—and not just because of the glaring similarities between the real-life Marcuses and the fictional Mantles. In March 1976, a long feature article by journalists Ron Rosenbaum and Susan Edmiston appeared in *Esquire* magazine. Its subject was the Marcus case. Its title was . . . "Dead Ringers."

The Marcus case became national news in the summer of 1975. In mid-July, residents of a luxurious high-rise on the east side of Manhattan noticed a fetid smell emanating from Cyril Marcus's tenth-floor apartment. A few days later, after the stench had grown unbearable, the cops were called. Breaking open the front door, they found a scene of unimaginable squalor—"the filthiest place I ever saw," according to one veteran police sergeant. The living-room floor was blanketed with empty beer cans, rotting chicken-salad sandwiches, half-eaten containers of moldering take-out food, clumps of human excrement. Flies darted everywhere. There were also more than fifty empty vials of Demerol, Nembutal, and other addictive drugs.

But it was the bedroom that held the ghastliest sight. There, sprawled across the mattress of one of the twin beds, was the corpse of Stewart Marcus. He was naked except for a pair of blue-striped shorts, and his blackened, bloated face was decomposed almost beyond recognition. Cyril—whose face was distinctly less decayed than his brother's—lay stretched on the floor at the foot of the second bed.

The ghastly discovery inside Apartment 10H became an instant, front-page sensation. FIND TWIN DOCS DEAD IN POSH PAD blared the headline of the next day's *Daily News*. Several factors made the story irresistibly titillating—perfect fodder for the tabloids. First, there was the sheer, grotesque creepiness of the case—the fashionable Upper East Side apartment that proves to be a chamber of horrors, containing the decomposing corpses of naked identical twins. Second, there was the stature of the victims themselves. The Marcuses weren't just any physicians, but world-famous fertility experts who had authored a standard textbook in their field and were worshiped as miracle workers by their upscale clientele. Mostly, however, there was the awful mystery surrounding their deaths—the bewildering question of how two such brilliant and accomplished men could have come to such an appalling end.

As investigators dug into the extraordinary life and terrible death of the Marcus twins, a picture emerged of two inseparable siblings who, after a lifetime of sterling achievement, had undergone a sudden, inexorable descent into madness and self-destruction. They were born in June 1930 (under the sign of Gemini, the Twins). Like the fictional Eliot Mantle, Stewart was a few minutes older than his brother. Throughout their lives, the smooth-talking, extroverted Stewart would be the dominant member of the duo, while Cyril—reserved and self-effacing— would play second fiddle.

From the time they were children, their lives were so intertwined that (according to one source discovered by Rosenbaum and Edmiston), "if one of them got into mischief, both were spanked by their mother to be sure that the right one was punished." They did everything together. In high school, when Stewart ran for class president, Cyril ran for treasurer. And their successes would go hand in hand, too. At graduation, Stewart became valedictorian; Cyril (always slightly subordinate to his brother) was named salutatorian.

As their education proceeded, so did their lifelong pattern of togetherness. As Rosenbaum and Edmiston sum it up: "Same college (Syracuse). Same fraternity. Same academic honors. Same medical school (also Syracuse). Shared the same cadaver in first-year anatomy class. Same medical honors. Same residency in gynecology at Mt. Sinai."

Much against their wishes, they were compelled to endure a three-year separation during their residencies—the only time in their lives when they would live apart. Afterward they joined up again for good, running both the infertility clinic at New York Hospital and a private practice catering to a Park Avenue clientele. As in Cronenberg's movie, the "older" twin—Stewart—was the suave, smooth-talking extrovert who handled the more glamorous tasks, from fund-raising to speechmaking, while the reserved, self-effacing "baby brother"—Cyril—took care of the more mundane business.

Things started to go bad around 1970. The breakup of Cyril's marriage plunged him into a deep depression. Two years later, he suffered a major collapse—possibly from a stroke. Locked in a monstrous symbiosis with his brother, Stewart began to deteriorate at around the same time. Soon their careers took a downward turn. "Patients began to report instances of bizarre, even terrifying behavior," report Rosenbaum and Edmiston. "One twin would leave his patient in the middle of an examination and the other would return to the stirrups to complete the job." They would "become irrationally angry and blow up at their patients," or—alternately—engage them in long, rambling, often bizarre conversations. On one particularly harrowing occasion, Cyril—scheduled to perform surgery—staggered and collapsed on his way to the operating room "in a way that suggested he was under the influence of drugs."

As the twins began to behave more and more erratically, their supervisors at the hospital forced them to take a leave. Ultimately, they retreated into Cyril's apartment, where—trapped in a spiraling madness—they subsisted on root beer, ice cream, and drugs. Their deaths were evidently very similar to the ones met by the Mantles in *Dead Ringers* (though without the typically Cronenbergian touch of grisly disembowelment). According to Rosenbaum and Edmiston's reconstruction, sometime around July 10, 1975, the two decided to commit double suicide and ingested large amounts of Nembutal. Stewart died as planned, but Cyril somehow survived. Awakening hours or even days later, he made one last desperate effort to escape, stumbling out of the apartment and encountering the doorman, who would later report that Cyril (by that time down to one hundred pounds) "looked like death." But—as in *Dead Ringers*—the younger twin immediately realized that he couldn't exist without his other half. Returning to the apartment, he locked himself inside and perished in the company of his twin's rotting corpse. Ultimately, the cause of Cyril's death was apparently nothing less than the impossibility of separation from the being to whom he had been so profoundly—and fatally—conjoined.

Dirty Harry

Real life often has an annoying habit of not tying up all its loose ends. But then that's one of the reasons we have *reel* life, to supply clear-cut, satisfying conclusions to distressing situations. Few movies have delivered this sort of payoff as well as this classic cop action film.

In 1971, violent crime was on an upswing, and many Americans were frustrated by the seeming inability of the police and the courts to make a dent in the problem. Then Clint Eastwood, in the guise of Dirty Harry Callahan, strode across the movie screen to offer a distinct, if severe antidote. Reckless robbers and vicious murderers did not get away from him, and once caught, no legal technicality could protect them. One way or another Dirty Harry put them in their place, often a place six feet under. Directed by the great action *auteur*, Don Siegel, the film obviously tapped into anxieties about the crime rate in general, but also about one anxiety in particular, especially for viewers from Northern California. They knew very well that Dirty Harry was tackling a menace suggested by a real serial-murder case that had begun just three years earlier.

For ten months between 1968 and 1969, a mystery gunman known only as Zodiac murdered five young people and wounded two others in the San Francisco Bay Area. He would seem to come out of nowhere, typically targeting couples on a date, and then would vanish without a trace. Panic seized the region. The killer taunted police with bizarre public letters, but law enforcement officials could never track him down. Eventually, Zodiac simply faded away. His crimes stopped, but no one ever succeeded in identifying him. In *Dirty Harry*, a crazed sniper, played to maniacal perfection by Andy Robinson, terrorizes San Francisco. Like Zodiac, he writes letters as a way to gloat over his atrocities and announce crimes to come. Also like Zodiac, he sports an astrological moniker—Scorpio. He differs from Zodiac in one important way. He has to contend with a .44 Magnum–toting Clint Eastwood. The citizens of *Dirty Harry*'s San Francisco, unlike the citizens of Zodiac's San Francisco, could rest assured that the case would end without any troubling uncertainties.

Zodiac came out of the night to claim his first victims on December 20, 1968. Two teenagers, David Farraday and Betty Lou Jensen, were parked on a lonely road outside the Bay Area city of Vallejo. Suddenly a man appeared outside the driver's-side window. In his hand was a .22-caliber automatic pistol. A shot to the head killed Farraday. Jensen tried to run but five bullets to the back brought her down. For half a year, the killer held himself back, then in July the Vallejo police received a mysterious call in the early hours of the morning. The caller directed them to a car in Blue Rock Springs Park where they would find two gunshot bodies. The caller added, "I also killed those kids last year." The information turned out to be accurate. In the park, the police found a nineteen-year-old boy, who was shot four times but would survive, and his twenty-two-year-old female companion, who would die on arrival at a nearby hospital.

Informing the police of his deadly exploits was not enough for the gunman. At the end of July he sent coded letters to three local newspapers. Each letter comprised a third of the murderer's message. Once deciphered, the notes provided a chilling glimpse into a deranged mind. "I like killing people because it is so much fun," the gunman explained, but there was also another, quasi-mystical reason for the murders. The killer believed that "when I die I will be reborn in Paradise and all I have killed will be my slaves." At the bottom of each letter was a cross drawn over a circle, the Zodiac symbol, providing a cryptic name for the serial murderer.

Zodiac attacked another couple that September. He wore a black hood entirely concealing his head except for two small holes cut out to allow him to see. On the lower part of the mask was the Zodiac symbol. For reasons that we will never know, he now dispensed with his pistol and instead assaulted the couple with a knife. He stabbed the young man five times, but not fatally, and killed the young woman with fourteen wounds. A month later he resorted to gunplay once again when he fatally shot a San Francisco cabdriver in the back of the head. This would be the last of his murders. He continued to post letters to newspapers, one of which contained his most ominous words yet: "School children make nice targets. I think I shall wipe out a school bus some morning." Fortunately, Zodiac never carried out this plan. Perhaps he was incarcerated in either prison or a mental hospital for some reason other than his murders. Or perhaps he committed suicide, presumably to be waited upon by his victims-turned-slaves. The Zodiac killings have never been solved. *Dirty Harry*, though, provided its own fictional coda to the case.

At the end of the film, Scorpio, Harry Callahan's nemesis, actually follows through on Zodiac's final threat: he hijacks a school bus full of children, clearly prepared to kill his hostages. Dirty Harry, of course, overtakes him and manages to separate the maniac from his helpless captives. After a long foot chase, Scorpio, despicable to the end, grabs a boy who happens to be fishing nearby and uses him as a human shield. He demands that Callahan drop his gun. In the real world, of course, the cop would probably have to comply, but this is Clint Eastwood acting out a classic piece of Hollywood wish fulfillment. The true-life Zodiac case had no clear resolution, leading to jittery theories that the murderer may have moved on to other killing grounds in other parts of the country. In *Dirty Harry*'s reel world, though, a miraculously aimed .44-caliber gunshot just above the hostage's shoulder brings the Scorpio murders to a most definite end.

Double Indemnity

"**W**e're gonna do it, and we're gonna do it right. There's not going to be any slipups—nothing sloppy, nothing weak. This is going to be perfect, straight down the line."

So says sleazy insurance salesman Walter Neff (Fred MacMurray) to Phyllis Dietrichson (Barbara Stanwyck), his steamy coconspirator in Billy Wilder's classic film noir, *Double Indemnity*. And, in fact, the two illicit lovers—who plot to murder Phyllis's abusive hubby and collect on a life insurance policy that pays double for accidental death—proceed with diabolical cunning. Every step in their elaborate scheme is carefully planned, then carried out with perfect coolness and precision timing. In the end, of course, the pair is outsmarted by a crack insurance investigator named Barton Keyes (Edward G. Robinson), who operates on the hunches supplied by the "little man" inside his gut. But even Keyes has to concede that the scheme cooked up by Walter and Phyllis is "as fancy a piece of homicide as anybody ever ran into—smart, tricky, and almost perfect."

The brilliant planning and cool resolve displayed by the murderous lovebirds in *Double Indemnity* is only one of many striking differences between the movie (based on James M. Cain's classic hard-boiled novel) and the real-life case that inspired the story. Far from being "smart, tricky, and almost perfect," the actual crime—involving a steely Queens hausfrau named Ruth Snyder and her Milquetoast loverboy, Judd Gray—was completely inept in both plotting and execution: a tragicomedy of errors that turned into one of the most sensational American murder cases of the twentieth century.

A voluptuous blonde with baby-blue eyes and a lantern jaw, Ruth Snyder was unhappily married to an overbearing art editor named Albert. Ruth, a perennial "party girl," had a craving for all the fun and excitement the Jazz Age had to offer. Her stick-in-the-mud mate, on the other hand, wanted a stay-at-home wife to cook, clean, and tend to his assorted domestic needs. Eventually, Ruth began seeking solace from her marital misery in the arms of assorted lovers.

In 1925, she was introduced to a mousy, myopic, thirty-two-year-old mama's boy named Judd Gray, who made his living as a corset saleman. Before long, they were involved in a torrid affair—meeting clandestinely in midtown hotel rooms, exchanging love letters composed in cloying baby talk, addressing each other by saccharine nicknames. To Judd, the domineering, brazenly sexual Snyder was his "Momsie"; she called her milksop paramour "Lover Boy."

One year after meeting Gray, Snyder resolved to do away with her detested husband. After tricking him into taking out a $48,000 life insurance policy with a double indemnity clause, she set about trying to kill him: spiking his whiskey with bichloride of mercury, sprinkling poison on his prune whip, piping gas into his bedroom while he slept. Snyder not only survived these attempts; in spite of his wife's barely disguised abhorrence, he apparently never suspected her.

Finally, the "Granite Woman" (as the tabloids would eventually dub her) decided to enlist her lover's help. Though Gray was genuinely appalled when his "Momsie" first broached the subject, he was helplessly in her thrall. (The tabloids would brand him the "Putty Man.") In the early hours of Sunday, March, 20, 1927, they put their plan into effect.

Fortified with enough bootleg liquor to intoxicate a dray horse and armed with a heavy iron sash-weight, Gray snuck into the Snyder home after dark, entering through a side door Ruth had left unlatched. When the victim was soundly asleep, Gray crept into the Snyders' bedroom and brought the bludgeon down on the sleeping man's head. The blow was so weak, however, that it only caused Albert Snyder to sit up with a roar and grab his assailant by the necktie.

"Momsie!" screamed Gray. "For God's sake, help!"

Rushing to the bedside, Ruth grabbed the sash-weight from her Lover Boy's hand and delivered a crushing blow to her husband's skull. Albert Snyder subsided onto the bed with a shuddering moan. For good measure, the assassins garroted him with a wire and stuffed chloroform-soaked rags up his nostrils.

Putting the second phase of their scheme into action, the pair proceeded to ransack the house to make it look as if Snyder had been killed in the course of a break-in. They upended furniture, opened drawers, even ripped the stuffing out of pillows. Ruth wanted Gray to make off with her jewels, but—for unexplained reasons—he refused. They settled for hiding her valuables under her mattress and stashing her fur coat in a bag inside her closet. Their clever idea for disposing of the bloody murder weapon was to rub it with ashes and stick it in Albert Snyder's basement tool chest.

Though Ruth urged Gray to knock her unconscious, he couldn't bring himself to hurt her. Instead, he bound her wrists and ankles, gagged her with cheesecloth, and made off into the night.

A few hours later, at around, 7:30 A.M., Ruth dragged herself to her sleeping daughter's bedroom and managed to rouse the eleven-year-old child, who immediately summoned help. Though Ruth stuck to her pre-rehearsed story, police were wise to her from the start. All the evidence was against her. Burglars are not known for knocking over armchairs and tearing open pillows in their search for booty. And Ruth's claim of being knocked unconscious by the intruder failed to persuade the medical examiner, who was unable to detect a single contusion on her scalp. Her cause wasn't helped when detectives turned up her "stolen" jewelry underneath her mattress, found the bloodstained murder weapon in her husband's tool chest, and discovered a tie tack with the initials "J.G." at the foot of Albert Snyder's bed. The bumbling conspirators were in custody within twenty-four hours.

The Snyder-Gray case became an immediate *cause célèbre*, not only in America but throughout the world. Ruth Snyder instantly became the most reviled woman of her time—the Whore of Babylon in the guise of a buxom Queens housewife. The Snyder-Gray trial—attended by such Jazz Age celebrities as David Belasco, D. W. Griffith, Sister Aimee Semple McPherson, the Reverend Billy Sunday, Damon Runyan, Will Durant, and others—received almost as much attention as the Lindbergh flight and was rich in both lurid melodrama and coarse comedy, particularly when Ruth was on the stand. (In one memorable exchange Assistant District Attorney Charles W. Froessel—trying to establish Ruth's earlier affair with a man named Lesser—asked, "Did you know Mr. Lesser carnally?" "Yes," Ruth replied. "But only in a business way.")

Public sentiment was so inflamed against Ruth that—after she and Gray were convicted and sentenced to death—every member of the court of appeals received a copy of the following postcard:

COURT OF APPEALS, QUEENS COUNTY
JUDGES:
   We will shoot you if you let that Snyder woman go free. She must be electrocuted. The public demands it. If she is not done away with, other women would do the same thing. She must be made an example of. We are watching out.
                                                            THE PUBLIC

The public got its wish. Shortly after eleven P.M. on Thursday, January 12, 1928, Ruth went to the chair, followed eight minutes later by Gray. As it happened, one of the witnesses, a *New York Daily News* reporter named Thomas Howard, showed up at the execution with a small camera secretly strapped to his ankle. Casually crossing his leg, he waited until the executioner threw the switch, then released the shutter button with a cable that ran down his pants leg. The resulting photograph—a blurry shot of Ruth Snyder's body, stiffening as the current coursed through it—was featured on the front page of the *Daily News*, becoming the most infamous picture in the history of tabloid journalism.

THOMAS HOWARD: PICTURE SNATCHER

The Ruth Snyder–Judd Gray case spawned not only *Double Indemnity* but a nifty little film called *Picture Snatcher*. Released in 1933, the movie stars James Cagney (in a typically high-voltage performance) as an ex-con named Danny Kean. Following his release from Sing Sing, Danny becomes a daredevil cameraman for a sleazy New York City tabloid. He scores his biggest coup when—after learning that an infamous murderess is about to be electrocuted—he sneaks into the prison with a camera hidden under his pants leg and snaps a picture of the prisoner at the instant of her execution. When the photo is plastered on page one of the next day's paper, the issue becomes a sellout (though Danny suffers some unfortunate personal consequences, since the security guard he has managed to sneak past—and who is demoted as a result—is none other than his girlfriend's father.)

The character of Cagney's hustling, anything-for-a-scoop "picture snatcher" was based on the real-life cameraman Thomas Howard, who took the infamous photo of Ruth Snyder's execution that ran on the front page of the January 13, 1928, issue of the *Daily News*. Howard's notorious feat was also the basis for a 1942 B-movie remake of *Picture Snatcher* called *Escape from Crime*.

The English Patient

In **a stunning** display of dramatic versatility, the superb British actor Ralph Fiennes—who had audiences hissing him as the hateful Nazi commandant in Steven Spielberg's *Schindler's List*—turned himself into an international heartthrob as the tragic title character in Anthony Minghella's Academy Award winner, *The English Patient*. Indeed, Fiennes literally went from one extreme to the other—from the personification of pure evil in Spielberg's film to the embodiment of sheer romantic love in Minghella's. As the dashing, doomed Count Laszlo Almasy, Fiennes instantly became the hottest screen actor to roam the desert sands since the days of Rudolph Valentino.

Told largely in flashbacks, Minghella's film—boldly adapted from Michael Ondaatje's Booker Prize–winning novel—focuses on the horribly disfigured title character, a Hungarian nobleman and explorer who, before the outbreak of World War II, had been part of a team of cartographers, mapping the uncharted sands of the North African desert as part of a Royal Geographic Society expedition. Prior to the incident that turned him into "toast" (as he puts it), Count Almasy—a haughtily remote, emotionally repressed man with little use for social niceties—had fallen violently in love with the radiant Katherine Clifton (played by Kristin Scott Thomas), wife of another expedition member. When her husband, Geoffrey, discovers his wife's infidelity, he attempts to end all their lives by aiming his biplane at Almasy. Though Geoffrey manages to kill himself in the crash, he succeeds only in injuring Katherine (a passenger in the two-seater plane), while Almasy escapes unscathed.

Bearing his wounded lover in his arms, Almasy carries her across the desert to the refuge of a cave, where he lights a fire, leaves her with a supply of water and food, then marches off for help. Arriving three days later at a British army outpost, he is mistaken for a German spy and placed under arrest. Eventually, he manages to escape. Making his way back to Katherine, he encounters a troop of German soldiers and trades them a portfolio of his precious desert charts for the use of a biplane. By the time he arrives at the cave, however, Katherine is dead. Loading her body into the plane, he takes off for the skies, only to be shot down by German antiaircraft artillery. Now, dying in a ruined Tuscan monastery—his once beautiful face a ghastly mask of scar tissue—he dwells obsessively on memories of the fiery affair that led to so much ecstasy and horror.

That someone as passionate, gallant, and matinee-idol handsome as Fiennes's Almasy could really exist is hard to believe. And in fact (as is so often the case) the truth is considerably less glamorous than the fiction. Yes, there really was a Count Laszlo Almasy who served as the basis for the hero of *The English Patient*. But in many ways, the actual Almasy was probably closer to the character Fiennes portrayed in *Schindler's List* than to the model of manly perfection he played in Minghella's film.

Born in Hungary in 1895, the real Count Almasy—like his fictional counterpart—was, indeed, an intrepid, globe-trotting, multilingual explorer who led an exceptionally adventurous life. But far from contracting a star-crossed and disastrous passion for another's man's wife, the actual Almasy (a skinny, hollow-chested man with bad teeth) was a lifelong homosexual. The great love of his life appears to have been a young German army officer, to whom he wrote dozens of deeply passionate letters, about eighty of which still exist. Nor did Almasy die after being horribly disfigured in a plane crash while transporting his dead lover's body across the skies of war-torn North Africa. He lived until he was fifty-five, dying of dysentery in Austria in 1951.

In the movie, Almasy—deep in the throes of his all-consuming passion—ends up aiding the Nazis only as a way of being reunited with his love. By contrast, the real Almasy was a rank opportunist who was willing to help anyone who suited his purposes at the moment. In the 1930s, he offered his services to British intelligence, but was turned down because he was suspected of being pro-German. He tried the Italians next, but they weren't interested, either. After the war, he informed for the Soviets.

The bulk of his espionage work, however, was performed for the Nazis. In a 1996 *New York Times* article, "The Real Hungarian Count Was no 'English Patient,'" reporter Jane Perlez summarizes Almasy's perfidious career:

> The real Count, known for his intimate knowledge of the North African desert, was specifically requested in 1940 from the Hungarian government, then sympathetic to though not officially allied with Germany, by the German military for work with [Field Marshal] Rommel . . . For a while, Almasy was in Berlin, then transferred to the desert headquarters.
>
> Awarded the rank of major in the German Air Force, the Count made a number of audacious raids. Driving a captured British Ford car through British lines in the North African desert, he traveled nearly 2,000 desert miles, relying on water holes he knew from his expeditions in the 1930s, to take the infamous German spy, Hans Eppler, to an oasis near Cairo. In a mission code-named Operation Condor, Eppler was then able to set up a German intelligence headquarters in a houseboat on the Nile.
>
> The Count also made two daring though unsuccessful

attempts to get the pro-German head of the Egyptian Army, Masri Pasha, out of Egypt so that the Pasha could help Rommel take Egypt.

In another example of the real Count's treachery, Elizabeth Pathy Salett, the daughter of a Hungarian diplomat posted in Egypt in the 1930s, said that the Count had planned a desert museum as a front for German espionage.

So daring and valuable was his espionage work for the Nazis that Rommel himself (whom Almasy lauded in his 1943 book, *With Rommel's Army in Libya*) awarded him the Iron Cross.

The author of *The English Patient*, Michael Ondaatje, has said that he knew the real Count Almasy "may have been a spy or double agent." But for the purposes of his novel, he ignored those aspects of the story, focusing only on Almasy's exploits as an explorer, a man "transfixed by the desert." To some critics of *The English Patient*, however, portraying a Nazi sympathizer and collaborator in such a romanticized light makes the book (and the film) "amoral and ahistorical." According to Elizabeth Pathy Salett—whose father, a Hungarian diplomat, had been betrayed by Almasy—*The English Patient* is guilty of trivializing "the significance of the choices men like Almasy made."

For the average filmgoer, however, the politics of *The English Patient* are secondary to its power as one of the most satisfying cinematic love stories of modern times. We suspect that most viewers would agree with film critic Liz Braum, who wrote in the *The Toronto Sun:* "Because the movie is based on a fairly esoteric novel, it's tempting to over-analyze the goings-on. Oh, let's not. What we have here is great movie-making. Have a nice time."

The Exorcist

The cinematic version of William Peter Blatty's supernatural thriller—about a chubby-cheeked, prepubescent girl who gets possessed by an ancient Babylonian demon named Pazuzu—hit theaters on the day after Christmas, 1973. The novel, originally published two years earlier, had been a national bestseller, but the movie immediately turned into something else—a genuine cultural phenomenon that broke box office records and incited an outbreak of mass hysteria that *Newsweek* magazine (in a cover story on the subject) dubbed "The Exorcism Frenzy."

Brilliantly directed by Hollywood whiz kid William Friedkin (who had won an Oscar for *The French Connection*) and full of hair-raising effects by makeup maestro Dick Smith, the film was a truly harrowing experience. In the course of her ordeal, the adorable twelve-year-old victim is transformed into a grotesque, obscenity-spouting horror who spews pea-green projectile vomit at a priest, swivels her head 360 degrees, and, in one notorious sequence, masturbates with a crucifix.

These and other equally alarming scenes had an extraordinary effect on audiences (who turned out in such droves that, in some places, people had to stand on line for more than four hours just to buy tickets).

Everywhere the movie was shown, grown men and women passed out, got sick, or went berserk. One midwestern theater owner reported that "two to five people have fainted in here every day since this picture opened." Another complained that his janitors were "going bananas wiping up the vomit." In Berkeley, California, a male viewer threw himself at the screen in an attempt to "get the demon"; while in Toronto four women were so traumatized by the movie that they reportedly had to be institutionalized. Even those less severely affected by the film often found it so nerve-racking that they had to keep telling themselves "It's only a movie, it's only a movie, it's only a movie."

There was just one problem with this reassuring litany. The events depicted in *The Exorcist* weren't fictional at all. They were based very closely on real life.

Author William Peter Blatty was an undergraduate student at Georgetown University in 1949 when his attention was caught by a page-one story in the August 20 issue of *The Washington Post*. PRIEST FREES MT. RANIER BOY REPORTED HELD IN DEVIL'S GRIP read the headline. The story concerned a fourteen-year-old Maryland boy (pseudonymously identified as "Robbie Mannheim") who had presumably been the victim of demonic possession. He was eventually cured by an elderly Jesuit priest named William Bowdern after an arduous exorcism ritual that lasted nearly two months.

Fascinated by the story, Blatty originally hoped to write a factual account of the exorcism but abandoned the project after the publicity-shy Bowdern refused to cooperate. Instead, Blatty began to think of the case as the basis for a novel. Even as he pursued a career as a successful Hollywood screenwriter (whose credits eventually included Peter Sellers's popular "Inspector Clouseau" movie *A Shot in the Dark*), Blatty continued working on the novel. It took him fifteen years to complete it. After the phenomenal success of *The Exorcist* in both its printed and cinematic forms, the full details of the Mannheim case eventually became known to the public.

Originally from St. Louis, the Mannheims were a middle-class family who had moved to suburban Mt. Ranier, Maryland, not far from Washington, D.C. In January 1949, fourteen-year-old Robbie—whose favorite aunt, a devotee of spiritualism, had taught him how to use a Ouija board to communicate with the "Other Side"—underwent a string of weird experiences. Night after night, strange scratching noises came from behind his bedroom walls. Various pieces of furniture—tables, chairs, his bed—seemed to move by themselves. A painting of Christ on his grandmother's bedroom wall began to tremble violently.

Following the sudden death of his aunt on January 26, Robbie's personality underwent a dramatic deterioration. He became sullen, agitated, withdrawn, and was plagued by terrible nightmares. Eventually, his parents turned to their minister, the Reverend Schultz—himself a believer in parapsychology, telekinesis, and other pseudoscientific phenomena. Schultz grew convinced that Robbie was the victim of poltergeists and suggested that the Mannheims speak to a priest. "The Catholics know about things like this," he told them.

Taking their minister's advice, the Mannheims consulted a local priest, Father E. Albert Hughes, who—after interviewing Robbie— became convinced that the boy was under the influence of evil forces. Robbie was admitted to Georgetown Hospital, where, according to several accounts, he began muttering curses in an ancient language. Ugly red markings appeared on his body. Some were shaped like the devil; others took the form of sinister communications. At one point, while Father Hughes was at his bedside, the boy broke free of his restraints, ripped out a steel mattress spring, and slashed the priest's left arm from shoulder to wrist—a wound that required more than a hundred stitches.

Believing that he had met the devil and was no match for him, the young, recently ordained priest withdrew from the case.

Not long afterward the Mannheims took Robbie back to St. Louis, where he continue to display his bizarre, increasingly violent symptoms. Eventually, when all other forms of treatment failed, a fifty-two-year-old Jesuit priest—Father William S. Bowdern, pastor of St. Francis Xavier Church—was brought in for an exorcism. For two months, he subjected himself to a "black fast" of bread and water to prepare himself for the ordeal. The exorcism—conducted according to the centuries-old prayer book the *Rituale Romanum*—began in March 1949.

Bowdern was assisted by a young friend, Father Bishop of St. Louis University, who kept a detailed diary of the ritual. Ultimately, a copy of this diary would come into Blatty's possession and serve as the primary source material for his book.

Most of the events that eventually found their way into *The Exorcist* are recorded in the diary—the hideous transformation of the child's features; the blasphemies uttered in a fiendish, guttural voice; the violent shakings of the mattress; the heavy furniture moving by itself; the gobs of bile hurled at the priests; the letter-shaped welts springing up on the young victim's torso; the writhings and rages and fiendish laughter.

Though the exorcism began at home, most of it was carried out in a Jesuit hospital where Robbie was transferred in late March. At the beginning of April—and very much to the outrage of the malevolent spirit occupying the boy—Robbie was baptized a Catholic. Finally, on the Monday after Easter, April 18, 1949, while Bowdern and Bishop stood at his bedside reciting their prayers, Robbie suddenly sat bolt upright. Through his mouth came a voice that identified itself as St. Michael. "I command you, Satan, to leave the body—*now!*" boomed the voice. At that instant, a loud report, like a gunshot, exploded in the room, and the demon departed forever. "Robbie Mannheim"—whose true identity has never been divulged—went on to become a successful, happily married man and father.

Though he stuck close to the facts of the "Mannheim" case, Blatty made the story even more sensational (and titillating) by turning the victim from an adolescent boy into a prepubescent girl. He also imported a number of details from other cases he had researched— most notably, the rotating head and body levitation. Only one scene came entirely from Blatty's florid imagination—the infamous crucifix masturbation.

There is one additional intriguing true-life fact related to the creation of *The Exorcist*. The character of Chris O'Neill—the caustic but big-hearted movie star whose daughter becomes the plaything of Pazuzu and who is played in the film by actress Ellen Burstyn—was reportedly based on Blatty's good friend Shirley MacLaine.

Frenzy

After his classic thrillers of the 1930s and 1940s (*The 39 Steps, Suspicion, Shadow of a Doubt, Notorious*, etc.), his elegant masterpieces of the 1950s (*Vertigo, Rear Window, To Catch a Thief, North by Northwest*), and his groundbreaking shockers of the early 1960s (*Psycho, The Birds*), Alfred Hitchcock went into a sudden, sharp decline, turning out a string of clinkers (*Marnie, Torn Curtain, Topaz*) that suggested he had lost his edge. *Frenzy*, released in 1972, was hailed by his admirers as a major return to form for the maestro.

The film focuses on an embittered loser named Richard Blaney who (like so many of Hitchcock's heroes) finds himself caught up in nightmarish circumstances. London is in the grip of fear. A serial sex murderer—nicknamed "the Necktie Killer" because of his MO (he strangles his victims with a tie after raping them)—is at large. Eventually, Blaney—a hard-drinking loose cannon whose ex-wife and girlfriend are both slain by the psycho—is wrongfully accused, arrested, and convicted. The real culprit turns out to be Blaney's chum, the outwardly amiable produce merchant Bob Rusk. The case is finally cracked by the soft-spoken Inspector Oxford (whose main preoccupation is getting a decent dinner from his dotty wife, an aspiring French cook who insists on using him as a culinary guinea pig).

With its inimitable mix of ingredients—dark comedy and macabre violence, sardonic wit and nail-biting suspense, psychological complexity and pure, pop entertainment—*Frenzy* seems like a sheer fabrication, concocted entirely out of classic Hitchcockian ingredients. The truth is, however, that much like *Psycho*, this work of apparent artifice was inspired by a real-life criminal case—a series of crimes that has never been officially solved.

Frenzy opens with a quintessentially Hitchcockian scene. As a blowhard politician makes a speech about pollution, promising that industrial waste products and other "foreign bodies" will be cleansed from the Thames, the naked corpse of a young woman—garroted with a necktie—comes floating onto shore. (Hitchcock himself makes one of his fleeting trademark appearances as a spectator in this scene.) The real-life case of the "Thames Nude Murders" officially began in essentially the same way, with the discovery, in February 1964, of a nude, asphyxiated female floating near Hammersmith Bridge. Two months later, the naked body of another young woman, a twenty-year-old prostitute named Irene Lockwood, turned up in nearly the same location.

Over the course of the next nine months, four more victims were found, bringing the official body count to six. (Many crime buffs believe that two earlier murders— including that of a twenty-one-year street-walker whose strangled, slip-clad body was found in the river in 1959— were the work of the same homicidal maniac.) Because all the victims were prostitutes, the killings evoked memories of London's most fabled serial killer. And because they were all found in the nude, the tabloids quickly baptized the unknown killer with the unavoidable punning nickname: "Jack the Stripper."

Though the Stripper did not go in for the kind of ghastly mutilation preferred by his infamous predecessor, his MO was, in its own way, every bit as grotesque. Though some of his victims were strangled, others had died of asphyxiation. Moreover, their front teeth were missing and semen was found in their throat. This combination of circumstances led police to theorize that they had been choked to death through forced, savagely violent fellatio.

Early in the police investigation, the case appeared to be solved when a fifty-four-year-old bachelor named Kenneth Archibald admitted to one of the killings. Eventually, however, he retracted his statement, explaining that he had made the confession because he was depressed. Since the murder spree continued while he was in custody, Archibald—however unstable—was clearly not "Jack the Stripper," and he was acquitted after a lengthy trial.

Police interviewed dozens of prostitutes, trying to get leads on any particularly kinky johns, but this avenue of investigation led nowhere. The real breakthrough came when members of the Metropolitan Police Forensic Laboratory found particles of automobile spray paint adhering to the flesh of several victims. The discovery led officials to speculate that the bodies may have been stored in a paint shop before disposal. Since all the women had been abducted between the hours of eleven P.M. and one A.M. and dumped between five and six in the morning, the police further surmised that the crimes had been committed by a night-shift worker.

Eventually, police located the shop where four of the victims had apparently been kept. (The shop was also close to the spot where the Stripper's final victim, a twenty-seven-year-old prostitute named Bridget O'Hara, had been dumped in some bushes.) Investigators were finally closing in on the killer when one of their prime suspects—a forty-five-year-old night-security guard whose rounds included the paint shop—committed suicide, leaving a note that said he couldn't "stand the strain any longer." Even today, no one knows for certain if this individual (whose identity has never been made public) was "Jack the Stripper." But his suicide coincided with the cessation of the murders, and as far as Scotland Yard is concerned, the case is permanently closed.

The Fugitive

At least once every decade, our country is transfixed by a murder case so sensational that it is invariably ballyhooed by the press as "The Crime of the Century." In the Roaring Twenties, it was the slaying of little Bobby Frank by juvenile "thrill killers" Leopold and Loeb. In the 1930s, it was the kidnapping-murder of the Lindbergh baby. During the heyday of the hippie movement, it was the butchery committed by the drugged-out members of the Manson cult. And in our own decade, it was the savage double slaying of O. J. Simpson's ex-wife, Nicole, and her waiter-friend, Ron Goldman.

During the 1950s, the murder case that generated the most intense fascination throughout the country involved a midwestern osteopath named Sam Sheppard, whose story became the direct inspiration of the hit TV series *The Fugitive* and the subsequent 1993 movie starring Harrison Ford. More than forty years after the brutal slaying of Sheppard's wife, Marilyn, the identity of her killer has still not been definitively established and remains one of the most tantalizing mysteries in the annals of American crime.

The murder that became a nationwide *cause célèbre* took place in the early-morning hours of July 4, 1954. The previous evening, Sam and Marilyn Sheppard—former high-school sweethearts who had been (to all appearances) happily married for almost ten years—had entertained another couple at their lakefront home in Bay Village, Ohio, an upper-class suburb of Cleveland. By the time their guests departed around midnight, "Dr. Sam"—who had spent an exhausting day at the private hospital he ran with his father and two brothers—had already conked out in the living room. Leaving her husband asleep, thirty-one-year-old Marilyn (an attractive brunette who was four months pregnant at the time) retired upstairs. Sound asleep in the next bedroom was the Sheppard's seven-year-old son, Samuel Reese, nicknamed "Chip."

Since all the suspects in the case are now dead, no one will ever know precisely what happened next. The story that Sam Sheppard would tell again and again, without ever deviating from its main details, was this:

Sometime in the middle of the night, he was awakened by the cries of his wife, who was moaning and calling his name. Drowsily, he made his way upstairs and, entering his bedroom, saw "a form with a light garment . . . grappling with something or someone." Suddenly he was struck from behind and lost consciousness.

When he came to, he was lying on the floor beside his wife's bed. Marilyn had been so savagely beaten that, even at a glance, he could tell that "she was gone." Her face was battered beyond recognition, her nose was broken, several teeth were missing. There was blood everywhere. It drenched the mattress and was spattered all over the walls and door. Later, police would also discover a trail of blood leading from the bedroom all the way down to the basement.

Dashing into his son's room, Sheppard found the boy fast asleep. Suddenly he heard a noise from below and bolted downstairs. The back door was open, and through it, he could make out "a form progressing rapidly toward the lake." It appeared to be a middle-aged man, about six feet, three inches tall, with dark bushy hair and a white shirt.

Chasing the fleeing figure across the lawn and down the wooden steps to the beach fifty feet below, Sheppard threw himself at the man and grabbed him from behind. After a brief, violent struggle, the thirty-year-old physician—a 170-pound six-footer who had been captain of his high-school football team—felt a "choking sensation" and lost consciousness.

Dawn was already beginning to break when he next came to. Staggering back into the house and upstairs to his bedroom, he checked his wife's pulse and determined that she was dead. At around six A.M.—after wandering dazedly about the house for a while—he called his neighbor, village mayor Spencer Houk. "For God's sake, Spen, get over here!" he cried. "I think they've killed Marilyn."

The first newspaper stories portrayed Marilyn Sheppard as the victim of a jewel thief who had beaten her to death when she discovered him in the act of ransacking her bedroom. According to these accounts, Dr. Sam had been severely injured by the intruder while coming to the rescue of his wife. Before long, however, Sheppard himself emerged as the prime suspect in the murder. According to the police, there were no signs of a break-in in the house. Though Sam had indeed suffered significant injuries—including a fractured vertebra in his neck—the notion that the athletic six-footer had been knocked out twice by the mysterious assailant seemed hard to swallow. And there were plenty of other suspicious elements, too: Sheppard's inability to account for the two-hour lapse between Marilyn's death and his call to Spencer Houk; the unaccountable disappearance of the white T-shirt he had been wearing when he fell asleep on the downstairs daybed; the fact that the family dog hadn't barked and that seven-year-old Chip had somehow slept through both his mother's savage murder and his father's supposed struggle with the "bushy-haired intruder."

Though he stoutly denied his guilt, Sheppard's case wasn't helped by his apparent reluctance to cooperate with police (he refused to take a lie detector test and immediately retained a well-known criminal attorney), or by the fact that—contrary to his assertions of marital devotion and fidelity—a young woman named Susan Hayes came forward and confessed that she and Dr. Sam had been conducting a torrid, long-term affair.

Within days, the case had turned into a full-fledged media circus, with Cleveland newspapers openly accusing Sheppard of the murder and demanding his arrest. QUIT STALLING AND BRING HIM IN ran the headline in one local paper. With an inflamed public already convinced of his guilt, Sheppard was taken into custody on July 29, 1954.

The outcome of his trial, which began in November, was a foregone conclusion. On December 21, after six weeks of testimony, the jury brought in a verdict of guilty in the second degree. Sheppard was given a life sentence by a judge who—even before the proceedings began—reportedly told a nationally syndicated columnist that the defendant was "guilty as hell. There's no question about it."

While Sheppard languished in the Ohio Penitentiary, his family kept up the fight to prove his innocence. In 1961, they retained F. Lee Bailey—then an ambitious young attorney who was determined to make a national name for himself. By April 1963, he had filed a petition in federal court, arguing that unbridled media coverage of the case had made it impossible for Sheppard to receive a fair trial. The following summer, in a stunning turn, Sheppard was released from prison by District Judge John Weinman, who agreed that Sheppard's constitutional rights had been violated by the irresponsible behavior of the press, which had turned his trial into "a mockery of justice." "If ever there was a trial by newspaper," he wrote, "this is a perfect example." Two years later, on June 6, 1966, the U.S. Supreme Court upheld Judge Weinman's findings, declaring that "the massive, pervasive, and prejudicial publicity attending petitioner's prosecution prevented him from receiving a fair trial consistent with the Due Process Clause of the 14th Amendment."

That fall—November 1966—the state of Ohio put Sheppard on trial again. Twelve years had passed since his original conviction and things were very different this time. For one, he was being represented very aggressively by one of the most colorful and effective defense lawyers of the age, F. Lee Bailey, who—in addition to his legal prowess—was a master of PR, and had managed to generate considerable sympathy for his client through the media.

Perhaps even more significant was the enormous popularity of the weekly TV drama *The Fugitive*, a top-rated prime-time program from 1963 to 1967. Dealing with the adventures of a wrongfully convicted physician, pursuing the shadowy "one-armed man" who had murdered his wife, the show was clearly based on the Sheppard case (with a bit of Victor Hugo's *Les Misérables* thrown in, in the form of a relentless policeman *à la* Inspector Javert.) The American public's deep sympathy for and identification with the program's hero, Dr. Richard Kimble, inevitably spilled over onto his real-life inspiration, Dr. Sam Sheppard.

On November 16, 1966, the jury brought in a not-guilty verdict. Sheppard was a free man, and F. Lee Bailey's reputation was made.

Sheppard's nightmare, however, hadn't really ended. Indeed, his life went into a dreadful spiral following his exoneration. Readmitted to the practice of medicine, he was sued for malpractice after the death of one of his patients. He took to alcohol and drugs. In 1968, the woman he had married while in prison divorced him, claiming that he had stolen money from her, threatened her life, and thrown bottles at her. He became—of all things—a professional wrestler (in a pre-Wrestlemania era, when a profoundly disreputable, freak show air hung about the so-called sport). In April 1970, he was found dead of liver failure. He was only forty-six years old.

In recent years, the case has been back in the news, thanks to the unremitting efforts of the now grown-up Samuel Reese Sheppard to establish, beyond any remaining doubt, that his father was innocent of the murder and that the "bushy-haired man" really existed. Employing modern-day DNA tests (unavailable at the time of the murder), experts have shown that the trail of blood leading from the bedroom to the basement of the Sheppard home belonged to a third party. Proof has also emerged that, contrary to the initial claims of the police, the lock on the basement door had, in fact, been tampered with.

The likeliest culprit, most people agree, was the Sheppards' window washer, a man named Richard Eberling, who ended up in prison after being convicted of bludgeoning an old woman to death. Eberling (who was familiar with the Sheppard home, fit the general description of the "bushy-haired intruder," and was arrested for robbery in 1959 with Marilyn Sheppard's diamond ring in his possession) certainly had both a motive and an opportunity. But the former window washer—who died in prison in August 1998—went to his grave denying that he had committed the murder. Samuel Reese Sheppard remains absolutely convinced of Eberling's guilt, but his efforts to have the state reopen its investigation have so far proved fruitless.

A TRULY GREAT ESCAPE

In March 1944, seventy-six captured airmen escaped from Stalag Luft 3, a German prison camp eighty miles southeast of Berlin. *The Great Escape,* the classic 1963 adventure film, was clearly based on this event, but the film straddles the fence when it comes to strict authenticity. On the one hand, the movie is based on a memoir of the escape, and an on-screen postscript states, "This picture is dedicated to the fifty," thus certifying that the Germans' murder of fifty recaptured prisoners at the end of the film was a reenactment of a real event. But then the movie does not use any of the actual names of the men involved in the spectacular 1944 breakout. Whether or not *The Great Escape* qualifies as an official recreation, one thing about the movie is certain: it is a stirring tribute to an epic flight to freedom, faithfully reproduced on screen in its most important details.

As is portrayed on screen, the prisoners at Stalag Luft 3 simultaneously dug three major escape tunnels, designated Tom, Dick, and Harry. The mastermind of the intricately planned operation was Roger Bushell, a South African attorney turned RAF squadron leader who came to be known simply as X (on film the corresponding character's name is Bartlett, code-named Big X, and is played by Richard Attenborough). Out of spare parts found around the camp, Bushell's organization cobbled together wooden tracks and trolleys running the length of the tunnels and air pumps to main-

(continued...)

A TRULY **G**REAT **E**SCAPE

tain a supply of oxygen for diggers working belowground. One of the biggest problems faced while working on the tunnels involved the disposal of the excavated dirt. A yellow-colored sand, it could not simply be dumped onto the gray topsoil where it would be easily spotted by guards. Fans of *The Great Escape* should already be familiar with the solution to this problem. Prisoners carried the sand in sacks concealed beneath baggy pants and strolled over to patches of overturned earth where prisoners were cultivating a garden. There the sand would be released. The gardeners finished the job by raking the sand into the soil. Also seen on film is the preparation for the escapees' eventual flight across Germany. A team of forgers created identification papers and travel documents, a painstaking process requiring that the prisoners duplicate typescript by hand with pen and ink.

After one of the tunnels was discovered and another turned into a storage space for sand, X and his men devoted all their efforts to tunnel Harry. According to the original plan, over two hundred prisoners were supposed to escape via this route, which measured 336 feet long. Unforeseen complications on the night of the escape drastically reduced this number. The first problem arose when the prisoners discovered that the tunnel was too short. Upon emerging from the exit hole, they would have to scramble across ten feet of open ground before reaching the cover of the surrounding woods. The final problem occurred when a guard stumbled upon the tunnel exit after seventy-six prisoners had escaped. In the end, only three made it to the safety of England (in the film, these three were portrayed by John Leyton, James Coburn, and Charles Bronson). Still, the escape organization had achieved its strategic objective, which was to distract the Germans from their war effort. All told, five million of Hitler's men were bogged down in the search for the escapees.

Aside from the name changes, *The Great Escape* takes one significant liberty with the facts. On screen, the escapees include such stalwart Americans as Steve McQueen, James Coburn, and James Garner. In reality,

(continued . . .)

A Truly Great Escape

no Americans made it through the tunnel. Many took part in the digging and the preparations, but in the fall of 1943, months before the escape, all American prisoners were transferred to a new prison compound. The filmmakers, though, can be easily forgiven for wanting to improve upon reality in this case. After all, if they had stuck slavishly to the facts, we never would have had the pleasure of watching Steve McQueen and his motorcyle hurtling over barbed-wire barriers under a hail of German gunfire.

The Gunfighter

One of the first of the so-called adult westerns, *The Gunfighter* (1950) focuses on a western badman's psychological turmoil rather than his shoot-'em-up exploits. Portrayed by Gregory Peck, the notorious Jimmy Ringo struggles to escape his bloody past. He hopes to reunite with his estranged wife and child, but upstart gunslingers keep dogging him, each one eager to make a name for himself as the man who outgunned the great Ringo.

Putting the story into historical context is a preface superimposed on the film's opening images: "In the Southwest of the 1880's the difference between death and glory was often but a fraction of a second. This was the speed that made champions of Wyatt Earp, Billy the Kid, and Wild Bill Hickok. But the fastest man with a gun who ever lived, by many contemporary accounts, was a long, lean Texan named Ringo."

From this, the viewer might conclude that the movie tells a true story. But there is a hitch here. True, there really was a famed gunfighter in the 1880s named Ringo. But his name was not Jimmy Ringo, it was *John* Ringo. In slightly disguised form, *The Gunfighter* crafts its own take on the John Ringo legend. According to western lore, Ringo was both a feared gunman and a handsome, tormented outcast, a "brooding Hamlet among outlaws," as one writer put it. These are the traits that found their way into the Gregory Peck characterization. Otherwise, though, the story is pure fiction. It's understandable that the screenwriters took this route. The real Ringo's life was so shrouded in mystery that a movie would have to rely heavily on imagination and speculation in order to present a coherent picture of the man.

For years, the basic facts of John Ringo's life eluded historians. Was his surname actually Ringo? Or was it Ringgold? Did he grow up in Texas, or Missouri, or California? And which story about his family should we believe? Did he come from southern gentility, or was he related, instead, to the considerably less genteel Younger brothers and James boys, the famous border outlaws? At the time *The Gunfighter* was filmed, none of these questions had been satisfactorily answered. Only recently has new research unearthed some of the facts.

The enigmatic gunfighter's name, as it turns out, truly was Ringo, and he was born on May 3, 1850, not in Texas, Missouri, or California, but in Indiana. At the age of fourteen, he did pass through Missouri with his family and eventually settled in San Jose, California. The Ringos were not Dixie aristocrats, but they were distantly related, after all, to the outlaw Youngers. According to traditional fanciful accounts, John Ringo received a college education. In actuality, his schooling was meager. The consensus seems to be that he was more literate than most frontier desperadoes, but that, of course, is pretty faint praise.

Historians have placed a young John Ringo in Texas in the mid 1870s. His violence there left at least some sort of trail. He became embroiled in a two-year-long feud that raged in the central Texas county of Mason, and contributed his own share of mayhem by killing two men. He was arrested twice as a result. Both times he managed to avoid conviction; in one case he escaped from jail. Soon he became the subject of some loose talk. The word got around that he had died. Perhaps his ability to arise from his rumored death figured into the beginnings of his legend.

Drifting out of Texas, Ringo may have wandered north to the Kansas cattletowns where so many other gunslingers were congregating in the late 1870s, but no notable exploits, alleged or verified, emerged from that period. It was the fabled Arizona boomtown of Tombstone that was the setting for most of the Johnny Ringo stories. The Gunfight at the OK Corral, between the Earp brothers and the Clanton-McLowery gang, is the centerpiece of the Tombstone legacy, but the struggle that preceded and followed that famous shoot-out was filled with many other confrontations, quite a few of them involving the mysterious Ringo. He was allied with the Clanton-McLowery gang and was perceived as a sort of defiant standard-bearer for the outlaws of the region.

Part of the dark appeal of the Ringo legend derives from the gunman's contradictory nature. On the one hand he was considered a gentleman outlaw with a sense of the tragic. A friend remembered Ringo reading a letter from one of his sisters and expressing profound remorse at his becoming the prodigal son of such a fine family. On the other hand, he was also known for his fierce violent outbursts. In December 1879, for instance, Ringo met up with a man named Louis Hancock in a saloon north of Tombstone. Striking up a conversation with the man, Ringo offered to buy him a whiskey. Hancock insisted on drinking beer. Miffed by the man's drinking preference, Ringo shot him through the neck.

Ringo's counterpart in the Earp camp was the volatile Doc Holliday, the tubercular Georgia dentist turned gambler and gunman. Once, Ringo encountered Wyatt Earp and Holliday on the streets of Tombstone and challenged Earp to a showdown. Earp was not one to take foolish chances. He walked away. But Holliday eagerly took Ringo up on his offer. According to one version of this episode, the two triggerhappy badmen agreed to what was known at the time as a handkerchief duel. They would each grab an end of a handkerchief—which would place them within veritable point-blank range of one another—and then they would go for their guns. Town officials intervened, though, and broke up the confrontation before bullets could fly.

In an incident that helped establish Ringo's outlaw bravado, he once faced down two Earp brothers and Doc Holliday all at once—or so the story goes. At the time, Marshal Virgil Earp and his deputies, Wyatt and Doc, were riding to the nearby town of Charleston, where they planned to arrest one of Ringo's compadres, a rustler and stage robber named Curly Bill Brocius. Ringo got wind of this. He knew that the lawmen would have to cross a bridge to enter the town and decided to make his stand there. When the Earps and Holliday reached the bridge, Ringo was glaring at them from the other side, his rifle leveled and ready to fire. He tried goading the Earp party into crossing over, but they wanted no part of him. They turned around and rode back to Tombstone.

The shoot-out at the OK Corral left three of the Clanton-McLowery band dead. To even the score, their friends wounded Wyatt Earp's older brother Virgil, and murdered his younger brother Morgan. Ringo might have played a part in this killing. Wyatt certainly thought so and included Ringo among the men he intended to hunt down. In all, Earp found and killed three of the outlaws involved in his brothers' murder. Ringo eluded Earp, but he fell prey to other forces hounding him, personal demons that have never been explained.

The critical event may have been a visit Ringo made to his family in California. Apparently, his folks were not especially pleased to see the renegade Ringo, who had made such an infamous name for himself across the southwestern frontier. Soon after his return to Arizona, sometime in July 1882, he went on a monumental drinking binge. For days he drank and grew ever gloomier as he rode aimlessly across the region surrounding Tombstone. The bender finally came to end on the tenth day when John Ringo dismounted alongside a creek, sat beneath a nearby oak tree, and put a bullet in his head.

Over the years, the lack of hard facts about Ringo only seemed to fuel the imagination of western yarn spinners. In addition to appearances as a supporting character in such Wyatt Earp movies as *The Gunfight at OK Corral*, he got the full pop-culture treatment in the 1950s TV series, *Johnny Ringo*, starring Don Durant, and in the talking gunfighter ballad "Ringo," recorded by Lorne Greene. Neither of these has much to do with the real Ringo. The TV show, in fact, went so far as to portray him as a crusading lawman. In *The Gunfighter*'s Jimmy Ringo incarnation, at least, some attempt is made to dramatize the idea of a tragic, deadly desperado, haunted by memories of a family that he left behind.

THE GUNFIGHTER ■ 67

VIRTUAL WYATT

Every western fan knows that the movies have lavished a great deal of attention on real-life lawman Wyatt Earp. As the familiar story goes, Wyatt, with his brothers Morgan and Virgil and his tubercular gambler pal Doc Holliday, vanquished the notorious Clanton gang at Tombstone's OK Corral. In recognition of his exploits, Hollywood has assigned some of its most prominent leading men to portray him on screen. He has been played by Henry Fonda in John Ford's *My Darling Clementine,* by Burt Lancaster in *Gunfight at the OK Corral,* by James Garner in *Hour of the Gun,* and, during the early nineties, by both Kurt Russell and Kevin Costner in, respectively, *Tombstone* and *Wyatt Earp.* What some people, including western buffs, may not know is that Earp has several times appeared incognito on the movie screen as well.

In 1932, years before Earp became a horse-opera icon, a movie called *Law and Order* told the story of three lawmen brothers and their deadly sidekick who clean up a tough western town. The leader of the brothers, played by Walter Huston, is named Saint Johnson, and the sidekick, played by Harry Carey, is called Ed Brandt. Despite these misleading monikers, they are clearly fictional stand-ins for Wyatt Earp and Doc Holliday as they wipe out the town's outlaw gang in a climactic shoot-out at a stable, a substitute for the famous gun battle at OK Corral.

For years after this gritty early talkie, Earp would stride across the screen under his own name, but in the late fifties he would appear again in thinly disguised form. In 1957, when Burt Lancaster appeared as Earp in *Gunfight at the OK Corral* and Hugh O'Brian was achieving TV stardom in *The Life and Legend of Wyatt Earp*, B-movie *auteur* Sam Fuller came up with his own slant on the Earp legend. In *Forty Guns,* Fuller spun a western tale around surrogate Earps, the badge-wearing Bonnell brothers (Barry Sullivan, Gene Barry, and Robert Dix). Their enemies are the forty gunmen of the film's title, who come across as a fictionalized Clanton gang, although Fuller made one

(continued . . .)

Virtual Wyatt

very significant alteration. The gang's leader, rather than a mean and ugly Ike Clanton type, is played by Barbara Stanwyck, who complicates the issue of law and order with some simmering sexual tension between her and Barry Sullivan, the Wyatt-like Griff Bonnell.

Two years later, Earp returned in modified form once again, going under the name of Clay Blaisdell in the action-packed *Warlock*. Like Earp, he is an itinerant lawman assisted by a disreputable gambler-gunman. The fact that Blaisdell is played by Henry Fonda—already associated with the Earp character via *My Darling Clementine*—makes the connection even more striking. The Doc Holliday–like sidekick is portrayed by Anthony Quinn, who substitutes a club foot for the Holliday handicap of consumption. As was the case with *Forty Guns,* this quasi-Earp movie brings an offbeat element to the famed lawman's lore. Doc Holliday has typically been portrayed as a well-bred gentleman, fallen from grace, who redeems himself through his loyalty to Wyatt Earp. Quinn's almost-Holliday character, on the other hand, is not merely a steadfast compadre; his attachment to Blaisdell is so neurotic that he could pass for the lawman's closet would-be lover.

Guys and Dolls

Steely-eyed frontier lawmen rarely serve as the starting point for frothy MGM musicals. This 1955 songfest is an exception.

The official source for *Guys and Dolls* is the work of Damon Runyon, the great Broadway yarn-spinner who made lovable cultural icons out of gamblers, gangsters, and chorus girls. His short story "The Idyll of Miss Sarah Brown" was the primary basis for the film. In this tale, a Broadway gambler named Sky Masterson romances a beautiful Salvation Army worker. For students of western lore, the name of Runyon's hero should be a tip-off as to the original inspiration for the character. Baby Boomers who grew up watching cowboy TV shows should also be able to make an educated guess. Sky Masterson, played by Marlon Brando on screen, was modeled after none other than Bat Masterson, the legendary gunfighter and sheriff who once ambled down the dusty streets of Dodge City.

How exactly did Runyon extract the concept of a slick, citified gambler from the exploits of a western adventurer? Bat Masterson, after all, forged his reputation while hunting buffalo, fighting Indians, and running down frontier desperadoes. Images of the natty Brando sauntering across Times Square hardly spring to mind when considering this Wild

West résumé. But, in fact, there was more to Masterson's life. He primarily supported himself, like his fictional namesake, through gambling, and he did not confine his escapades to the western prairies and high country. At the turn of the century, he left the frontier behind and spent nearly the last twenty years of his life in New York City as, incredibly enough, a sportswriter. It was here that the young Damon Runyon met the famed western pistolero and began to formulate his own fanciful version of the man.

Bat Masterson first made a name for himself as a twenty-year-old buffalo hunter in the Texas Panhandle. In one of the most celebrated battles in western history, he and twenty-seven other men fought off an attack by a combined force of over one hundred Comanche, Kiowa, and Cheyenne warriors. Firing from inside the two-foot earthen walls of their hunting-camp sodhouses, they held out against one assault after another for two hours. Bat was regarded as one of the ablest defenders in this confrontation that could easily have served as a scenario for a western-movie climax. Two years later, in 1876, his reputation as a deadly gunman was reaffirmed when he killed a man in self-defense in the Texas town of Sweetwater.

Masterson was elected sheriff of Ford County, Kansas, in 1877. At the center of the county was Dodge City, the foremost and most rowdy of western cowtowns. Bat helped keep the peace and tracked down train robbers while rubbing shoulders with such frontier luminaries as Doc Holliday, Luke Short, and Wyatt Earp. In Dodge he also cultivated a taste for fine clothes, including the derby and silver-tipped cane that would later become the signature props for Gene Barry when he portrayed the western lawman on the *Bat Masterson* television series in the 1950s.

Most of Bat's time out west was spent moving from one boomtown to another, earning a living at poker, faro, and other games of chance. Eventually, Colorado would become his favorite stomping grounds. As a logical extension of this way of life, he took an interest in the then-burgeoning sport of prizefighting, first as a spectator and bettor, then later as a referee and purse-holder. In the latter two jobs, a gunman's reputation was helpful. A referee would sometimes have to stand up to a rough-and-tumble crowd displeased with a decision, and a purse-holder would have to discourage anyone who might covet the fight's winnings. Masterson's knowledge of boxing would later make it possible for him to segue into sportswriting.

Bat got his first taste of New York living in 1895. At the time, a mysterious letter writer was mailing death threats to a son of New York industrialist Jay Gould. At the advice of New York's chief of police, the Goulds hired Masterson as a bodyguard. As it turned out, Bat's duties primarily involved accompanying the younger Gould to the racetrack. He found big-city life, and big-city gambling, to his liking. He returned there for good in 1902.

For Masterson, Broadway amounted to the last of his boomtowns, full of the sort of colorful characters and nighttime attractions that he had always gravitated to. His job as a sportswriter for the *Morning Telegraph*, where he specialized in boxing stories, became a financial hedge against bad luck at the racetrack or the gaming tables. Quickly, he emerged as a premier figure on the New York gambling scene and in journalistic circles. His friends included cowboy movie star William S. Hart, up-and-coming reporters like Gene Fowler and Louella Parsons, and President Theodore Roosevelt. But as comfortable as Masterson got as an eastern urbanite, some old habits never left him—he still carried a revolver under his coat.

While he was a young newsman, Damon Runyon became friendly with the sheriff-turned-sportswriter. Bat Masterson may never have made a play for a Salvation Army doll (he was comfortably married at the time Runyon knew him) but Sky Masterson clearly shared some key traits with the old Dodge City lawman. As described by Runyon, he is, like Bat, a footloose gambler from Colorado who migrates from one wide-open town and one big game to the next, and he is a pistol-toting man-about-town who is not to be trifled with. As portrayed by Brando on screen, the Bat/Sky connection can most clearly be seen in the film character's integrity as a sporting man, the sort of guy who always deals square and never welshes on a bet.

In one critical respect, the original Runyon short story, unlike the film, diverges from the true spirit of Bat Masterson's life. At the end of

"The Idyll of Miss Sarah Brown," Sky embraces Miss Brown's straight-and-narrow ways and becomes a Salvation Army crusader himself. This Bat Masterson would most definitely never have done. He held fast to his life as a hard drinker and dedicated gambler until the day he died of a heart attack in 1921, slumped over his *Morning Telegraph* desk.

The Harder They Fall

Anyone looking for a dramatic lesson in the corruption and cruelty of the prizefighting game could not find a better example than the brief boxing career of Primo Carnera. A writer could not have invented a more telling scenario. All the elements are there: the lure of easy money, the exploitation of an innocent, the deception of the public, the savagery of the sport. Author Budd Schulberg had the most potent material to work with when he fictionalized the Carnera fiasco into an acclaimed novel, the source for this gritty 1956 movie.

The Harder They Fall was Humphrey Bogart's last film. His character represents one of the most significant differences between the Schulberg fiction and the Carnera fact. In an evocatively world-weary performance, Bogart plays a sportswriter who agrees to act as press agent for the crooked backers of Toro Moreno, a huge, lumbering Argentinian who is promoted into a heavyweight attraction, despite his complete ignorance of the boxer's craft. Bogart flacks for the cynical procession of fixed fights until finally he finds his employers' tactics so repellent that he exposes the entire scam. The character's belated moral stand brings a glimmer of hope to an otherwise grim tale. In the true story of Primo Carnera, there was no such hero and little moral consolation of any kind. Although quite faithful in spirit to its real-life inspiration, this movie diverges from the truth in one other respect as well. While Carnera was actually transformed into a heavyweight champion, the fictional Toro Moreno only makes it as far as heavyweight contention. Presumably, Schulberg had to scale back the tale to make it more plausible. The bare facts were too preposterous.

Primo Carnera was Italian rather than Argentinian. Otherwise, his background was virtually identical to Toro Moreno's. Like the boxer of *The Harder They Fall*, he came from a family of stonecutters and had once worked as a circus strongman. An awesome physical specimen, he measured six feet six inches tall and weighed over 260 pounds. The first parasite to market Carnera's oversized physique was a Frenchman named Léon See. In 1928, he brought Carnera to Paris, put boxing gloves on the strongman's ham-sized fists, and pitted him against a series of easily overcome opponents. Crowds rushed to see the Italian giant, made to seem even more gigantic by the Barnum-like See, who assigned undersized assistants to attend to him in the ring. See also made sure there were as many crowds as possible. Traveling from Paris to London, Carnera appeared in eighteen fights in just fifteen months.

One of the people who saw Carnera at this time was a New York wiseguy named Walter "Good Time Charley" Friedman. He concluded that Carnera could become an even greater success in America, provided that the strongman was handled by certain friends of his back in New York City. He brought Carnera to the United States and quickly attracted a syndicate of backers from the world of nightclubs and bootlegging, including George "Big Frenchy" DeMange, "Broadway Bill" Duffy, and Owney "The Killer" Madden. In a walkup apartment just off Broadway on West Forty-eighth Street, they schooled the ponderous Carnera in some of the fundamentals of professional pugilism. When he seemed to master the basic steps, the syndicate moved him on to his first American performance at Stillman's Gym, the mecca of prizefight training. There Carnera's larger-than-life proportions began to pay off. Two thousand spectators a day paid to watch Carnera spar. The public was intrigued by the hype that surrounded the strongman, who was characterized as a sort of Italian Paul Bunyan. According to press releases, each morning at breakfast Carnera consumed nineteen slices of toast, fourteen eggs, a half pound of ham, and an entire loaf of bread, washed down with a quart of orange juice and two quarts of milk.

The syndicate put Carnera, the so-called Ambling Alp, on the road in the early 1930s. If there was any doubt about the tour's lack of integrity, the number of fights alone should have been a tip-off. In nine months, Carnera compiled a staggering—one might say unbelievable—total of twenty-three victories. Carnera himself had no idea what sort of machinations were involved in orchestrating these matches. A simple, naive man, he believed that all these boxers were dropping to the canvas because of his awesome punching power.

Some writers have suggested that Carnera was not a completely incompetent boxer. Some say that he had good left jab, others contend that he moved well for a big man. But clearly he did not possess the skills of a contender, and according to sportswriter Paul Gallico, the improbable string of victories concealed an Achilles' heel: although Carnera could take a punch to the body, the merest tap on the chin in a real fight would be devastating.

For the syndicate, the greatest windfall in Carnera's rise to the top occurred when one of the strongman's opponents died in the ring. It's unlikely that Carnera actually had much to do with Ernie Schaaf's death. The critical damage had been inflicted earlier when Max Baer had landed one of his crushing rights to Schaaf's head, putting the boxer into a brief coma. Carnera, believing himself responsible, was guilt-stricken. His backers, meanwhile, reveled in all the publicity that the tragedy generated. (This episode is recreated quite faithfully in the film.)

Carnera got his title shot in the summer of 1933. When his opponent, Jack Sharkey, hit the deck on cue, the Ambling Alp became the world heavyweight titleholder. His reign did not last long. A year later, he faced Max Baer, the man who had inflicted such lethal damage upon Ernie Schaaf. (Bringing an extra touch of authenticity to *The Harder They Fall* is the appearance of Baer himself as Moreno's final opponent and as the boxer responsible for the earlier death in the ring.) What Carnera did not know was that this would be his first matchup against a real contender in an authentic fight. Baer knocked him down twelve times in eleven rounds before the referee finally brought the slaughter to an end and declared Baer the new champion. Soon after that, the syndicate's cruel abandonment of Carnera reached a new low when the Italian strongman faced a young Joe Louis. The future champ mauled Carnera so badly that the strongman ended up in the hospital.

While the syndicate was quick to cut Carnera loose, they remained very attached to their fighter's money. After payoffs, they pulled in around $700,000. Carnera saw precious little of that, and much of what he had seen he had sent back to his family in Italy. Penniless, he now returned home, as does Toro at the end of *The Harder They Fall*.

As bleak as Carnera's boxing career turned out to be, his fortunes improved somewhat after World War II. A promoter in Los Angeles groomed Carnera as a pro wrestler, a profession much better suited to his temperament and abilities. He now made a comfortable living and invested his money in a successful liquor store. He also appeared in several films. The most memorable was the original 1949 version of *Mighty Joe Young*. In this film, Carnera, playing himself, slugs it out with the oversized gorilla. He loses. But then, of course, the fight was fixed.

Stricken mortally ill in 1967, Carnera returned to his hometown of Sequals, Italy, where he died a short time later.

The Hills Have Eyes

When it was first released in 1977, this early Wes Craven film appeared to be a variation on the theme of *The Texas Chainsaw Massacre*. Like the cult power-tool hit from three years earlier, *The Hills Have Eyes* concerned a small group of defenseless travelers trapped in a southwestern wasteland by a family of blood-crazed psychos. In addition to the basic premise, the Craven movie's harsh look, insane violence, and dark humor were also clearly inspired by the earlier low-budget classic. Another inspiration, though, came from real life.

This true-crime basis, actually, represented another similarity with *Texas Chainsaw*, which had also been inspired by a real murder case, in particular, the outrages committed in the 1950s by Wisconsin ghoul Ed Gein. But anyone searching through modern criminal cases would have great difficulty discovering the model for Craven's mutant cannibal family that pounces upon unsuspecting wayfarers. The reason would be that the monsters of *The Hills Have Eyes* were patterned after an abominable clan who haunted the highlands of Scotland back in the early 1400s.

Craven's hill people were originally the victims of radioactive fallout produced by atom-bomb tests in the southwestern desert. The Beane clan of fifteenth-century Scotland, on the other hand, could not lay claim to any such mitigating explanation for their unspeakable crimes. From what we know about them, they appeared to have been merely ferocious throwbacks to an earlier Neolithic age.

Sawney Beane originally hailed from East Lothian county near Edinburgh on Scotland's east coast, where he grew up on his father's farm. Little else is known about his early years. As a young man he left the region, accompanied by his wife. Given his later escapades, it seems reasonable to assume that he left home under a cloud. Chances are it was a mighty dark cloud, dark enough to propel Beane and his wife some one hundred miles before finally stopping on Scotland's barren southwestern coast. They made their new home there in a cave at the base of a seaside cliff. It was obviously not a place for someone who intended to make his living from the land, as Beane's parents had done. Sawney would find sustenance by other means.

Feeding the Beane family was no small task. First Beane and his wife produced eight sons and six daughters. Then the children mated among themselves and produced another litter of Beanes. To feed this growing inbred family, Sawney and his clan resorted to desperate measures.

For twenty-five years, travelers disappeared from the lonely roads coursing through the southwestern highlands. Without a trace of these people left behind, inhabitants of the region had nothing but their imaginations to rely upon when attempting to explain the mystery. Perhaps man-eating wolves were on the prowl. Or maybe the culprits didn't belong to the natural world at all. The mysterious highlands, full of stark slopes and boggy valleys, might be infested with werewolves, some people thought. Or perhaps the vanishings were the work of Satan himself. No physical evidence was found to bring the theories back down to earth, although suspicion fell on certain people in the area from time to time. These suspects were summarily hanged. Still, the disappearances continued. According to one estimate, a thousand travelers vanished during those twenty-five years.

The truth came out one night in 1435. A group of people returning home from a nearby fair approached a bend in the road bordered by rocks and thicket. They heard a commotion up ahead. Rounding the bend, they came to a sudden stop and stared. Before them, a man and a woman had just been ambushed. The man was fighting for his life. The woman was nearby. On top of her were the attackers, so ragged and wild that they could only be described as savages. They had already cut the woman open. Now they were tearing off strips of flesh and devouring them.

There was a brief skirmish and then the cannibals fled into the hills, where they disappeared.

Word of the grisly incident reached Scotland's King James. He was so outraged that he took to the field himself and led a force of four hundred soldiers across the country to the area of the attack. As the troops searched along the rocky coastline, the hunting dogs picked up a scent. The trail led to a fissure in the base of the cliff and down through a watery, zigzag passageway. Finally the troops reached a cave—the home of Sawney Beane and his feral brood. There were forty-eight of them in all. The king's soldiers found a stash of stolen money and jewels. They also found, dangling from the ceiling, slabs of human flesh, as well as human arms and legs. Other cuts were pickling in a barrel.

Once the Beanes were herded back to the capital of Edinburgh, the authorities decided that there would be no trial. The Beanes were so far beyond the pale, they reasoned, that they didn't deserve the legal niceties enjoyed by normal human criminals. All that was left was to exterminate the creatures in an appropriate way.

In *The Hills Have Eyes*, the all-American family terrorized by the cannibals comes up with a series of ingenious, brutal methods for wiping out their tormentors. But their revenge could not compare with the retribution devised by Edinburgh authorities in 1435. First, the executioners chopped off the hands and feet of the twenty-seven Beane men. The Beane women were forced to watch as the males in their family slowly bled to death. That done, the twenty-one women were then all burned alive. If the case's most famous chronicler can be trusted, the Beanes did not express a great deal of remorse. In fact, they "continued cursing and venting the most dreadful imprecations to the very last gasp of life."

REEL TO "REAL" TO REEL?

This one's a little confusing, so pay attention.

In 1972, Wes Craven—whose name would eventually become permanently linked to the term "horror meister"—released his first directorial effort, a wildly sadistic little shocker called *Last House on the Left,* about a gang of psychos who torture and kill a pair of teenage girls, only to suffer a horrible retribution at the hands (and other body parts) of the parents of one of the victims. The ad campaign devised to promote this film was a masterpiece of cheesy exploitation. TO AVOID FAINTING, the ad advised, KEEP REPEATING IT'S ONLY A MOVIE . . . ONLY A MOVIE . . . ONLY A MOVIE . . . Filmgoers were understandably nonplussed, therefore, when the movie began with a title card assuring them that the events in the movie were based on real life!

In truth, however, *Last House on the Left* turned out to be a splatter-movie remake of Ingmar Bergman's 1959 classic, *The Virgin Spring.* Set in the Middle Ages, the film stars Max Von Sydow as a farmer whose daughter is brutally raped and murdered and who then exacts a horrible vengeance on her killer (who makes the boo-boo of taking refuge in the home of his victim).

In short, *Last House on the Left* wasn't (as the ads suggested) completely made up. Nor (as the film insists) was it based on real life. Rather, it stands as the only low-budget, exploitation gore flick ever to be based on an Academy Award–winning foreign film by one of world's greatest creators of highbrow art movies.

Hoosiers

"The Milan Legend has been kept alive and made important to America through *Hoosiers*. It's worth seeing every once in a while."

—Hilliard Gates, Indiana sports announcer

The premise of this *Rocky*-style sports movie is so wildly improbable (a bunch of earnest high schoolers from a minuscule midwestern town fight their way to the state basketball finals and win the championship on a last-second buzzer-beater) that it seems like a classic cinematic fairy tale—a pure, sugarcoated product of the Hollywood dream factory. But if you really *are* a Hoosier, then you know it's all basically true. The events depicted in this irresistible 1986 film are a thinly fictionalized version of one of the most celebrated stories in the annals of Indiana sports—the triumphant 1953–54 season of the high-school varsity basketball team from the tiny, southern Indiana town of Milan (pop. 1,100).

To say that Southern Indiana is basketball country is like saying that the Vatican is a religious community. Few things in life can arouse the passions of the local populace more intensely than the accomplishments of their high-school hoop teams. And back in the early 1950s, the good folks of Milan had plenty to get excited about.

At the end of the 1951–52 season, the team's venerable but autocratic coach, Herman "Snort" Grinstead, was canned by the school board and replaced with a young soft-spoken family man named Marvin Wood, who proceeded to alienate the town's many backseat coaches by introducing a whole new style of offensive play and—even worse—closing off practices to the public.

Even Wood's most disgruntled critics, however, were eventually won over as the Indians—led by their star guard, Bobby Plump—achieved the nearly impossible dream of making it all the way to the state finals. Though the Indians lost to the heavily favored team from South Bend Central, they were feted back home as heroes.

Given the magnitude of the achievement (in the entire, forty-plus-year history of Indiana high-school basketball, only a handful of Milan teams had ever progressed beyond local tournaments), no one expected the Indians to have another shot at the championship. But when they ran up an 18–2 regular-season record, it was clear that the Indians were serious contenders. They proceeded to win their second straight sectional title, then stunned observers by defeating the powerhouse Flying Tigers of Crispus Attucks High School, whose team included the young Oscar Robertson, arguably the greatest basketball player Indiana ever produced.

For the second year in a row, the "Cinderella team" from tiny Milan found themselves headed for the Final Four. So great was the occasion that the town fathers declared March 20, 1954—the day of the championship—a legal holiday, and urged everyone who could possibly make it to attend the big event.

The townspeople required little encouragement. When the big day arrived, Milan was a virtual ghost town. Almost every one of its 1,140 residents was at Butler Fieldhouse at Butler University—at that time, the world's largest indoor arena. The "Big Barn," as it was nicknamed, was crammed beyond its fifteen-thousand-seat capacity with journalists, sportscasters, and ordinary, basketball-crazed citizens, all in the grip of advanced "Hoosier Hysteria." An estimated 90 percent of all Indiana families were tuned in to the finals on radio or TV.

The game they witnessed exceeded their wildest expectations. Though the smart money was on the high-powered Bearcats of Muncie Central—a school that had won four previous state titles—the giant killers from Milan would not be denied. With only six seconds left in the game—and the score tied at 30—Bobby Plump dribbled the ball downcourt to the edge of the free throw line, faked, pulled back, jumped, and shot. The ball sailed through the hoop. With just three seconds left, the Bearcats could do nothing but try a last-second, desperation shot from beyond half-court, but the buzzer sounded before the ball was even released. Final score: Milan 32, Muncie 30.

Sheer pandemonium ensued. The "Mighty Men of Milan" became instant state heroes. Driving back home from Indianapolis, they were accompanied by a horn-honking procession thirteen miles long. More than forty thousand people lined the roads to cheer them as they passed. Bobby Plump, the player who made the "Shot Heard 'Round the World'" became a living Hoosier legend.

In 1986, *Hoosiers*—written by Indiana University graduate Angelo Rizzo, and directed by his former college buddy David Anspaugh—brought the Milan legend to the big screen. To be sure, the movie takes dramatic license with the truth, turning the head coach (Gene Hackman) into a deeply troubled figure, giving him a sexy love interest (Barbara Hershey), throwing in a town drunk who finds redemption through assistant coaching (Dennis Hopper), and adding a few other Tinseltown touches. And indeed, a number of Milan citizens have objected to what they call the "Hollywood hokum" in the film—the occasional swearing, the romance, the alcoholism.

Still, in telling the Cinderella story of the fictional 1951–52 "Hickory Huskers," the filmmakers captured the essence of the Milan Indians' miracle season. To ensure the authenticy of *Hoosiers*, key scenes were not only shot on location but featured numerous locals in both key roles and as extras. When the climactic tournament was shot at Hinkle (formerly Butler) Fieldhouse, the legendary Bobby Plump himself was present.

Bobby's buzzer-beating jumper completely transformed his life. Even today, he remains one of the most widely recognized figures in the state. The owner of a popular Indianapolis restaurant called Plump's Last Shot, he has recently penned a lively autobiogaphy, *Bobby Plump: Last of the Small Town Heroes*, which provides a rousing, game-by-game recreation of that fabled, long-ago season that is enshrined in Hoosier lore as the greatest sports saga of all time.

Inherit the Wind

As an ominous rendition of "Give Me That Old-Time Religion" blares from the soundtrack, four grim-faced men gather on a dusty, sun-drenched street and—like a band of gunfighters on their way to a showdown—march across town. Their destination, however, isn't the OK Corral but Bertram T. Cates's biology class at the local high-school. As a news cameraman sets up his tripod and shoots a photo, the earnest young instructor is placed under arrest. His crime: teaching evolution in violation of state law banning Darwinian theory from the classroom.

So begins Stanley Kramer's compelling, 1960 courtroom drama, *Inherit the Wind*, based on the hit Broadway play by Jerome Lawrence and Robert E. Lee. Set in the fictional town of Hillsboro, Tennessee— "the buckle on the Bible Belt"—the movie deals with the battle between fundamentalist religion and modern science. When news of Cates's arrest hits the papers, the town fathers worry that their little community will become a national laughingstock, a symbol of back-woods southern ignorance. But their concern turns to jubilation when they hear that the prosecution will be led by none other than Matthew Harrison Brady.

Former secretary of state under Woodrow Wilson and three-time presidential candidate, Brady (colorfully played by Fredric March) is a blustering tub of evangelical piety. His arrival in town is celebrated with a full-scale, banner-waving parade. To the good folk of "heavenly Hillsboro" (who are depicted as a bunch of Bible-thumping witch-hunters), Brady is nothing less than a savior—the champion of small-town decency and godliness, come to do battle against the dark forces of big-city atheism.

The incarnation of those evil forces (as far as the citizens of Hillsboro are concerned) is Brady's opponent, Henry Drummond, a celebrated Chicago lawyer described as "the most agile legal mind of the twentieth century." Whereas the whole town turns out to give Brady a hero's welcome, the rumpled Drummond (played with masterly understatement by Spencer Tracy) is greeted by only a single supporter—the cynical, wisecracking journalist, E. K. Hornbeck (Gene Kelly), whose Baltimore newspaper has put up the funds to bring Drummond in for the defense.

Set in July 1925, the action largely unfolds in a packed, stifling courtroom. As spectators and participants try desperately to cool themselves with handheld, palm-leaf fans, Brady and Drummond go head-to-head over the issue of religious faith vs. intellectual freedom. There is also a *Romeo and Juliet* subplot, involving the freethinking defendant, Bert Cates (appealingly played by Dick York), and his conflicted sweetheart, Rachel Brown, daughter of the town's frighteningly fanatical minister.

The film reaches its dramatic climax when Brady agrees to take the stand as a self-declared Bible expert. Under a merciless grilling by Drummond, the old man is exposed as a benighted buffoon, mindlessly clinging to archaic beliefs that no intelligent person could possibly hold (e.g., that the earth was created precisely 4,004 years before the birth of Christ). In the end, he is reduced to a state of stammering desperation and drops dead in the courtroom while delivering a last, ranting defense of his creationist credo. Though Cates has been found guilty, the victory clearly belongs to Drummond, who turns out to be not quite as godless as his enemies believe. In the final scene of the film, he takes both the Bible and Darwin's *The Origin of Species* in his hands, as though weighing them against each other. Then—stuffing them side by side in his briefcase—he marches from the courthouse to the stirring strains of "The Battle Hymn of the Republic."

The real-life basis of *Inherit the Wind* has never been a mystery, since its creators openly intended it as a thinly fictionalized version of the so-called Dayton "Monkey Trial" of 1925, one of the most famous legal proceedings of the twentieth century. For all their fidelity to historical fact, however, they also made some significant changes, partly for purely dramatic reasons, partly because of their ideological intent.

The opening scene of *Inherit the Wind*, for example—in which the courageous young biology teacher Bert Cates defies the bigoted town fathers and is hauled from the classroom like a common criminal—is completely fictitious. The actual "Monkey Trial" was a test case instigated by the American Civil Liberties Union in defense of academic freedom. After the Tennessee Legislature passed a bill prohibiting the teaching of Darwinian theory, the ACLU issued a press release, offering to defend any schoolteacher willing to challenge the law in court. This news item caught the eye of a Dayton, Tennessee, resident named George W. Rappleyea, a transplanted New Yorker who believed that there was no inherent contradiction between Christian faith and acceptance of Darwinian theory. Outraged over his adopted state's new antievolution statute, Rappleyea persuaded the town's civic leaders that drowsy little Dayton (which had suffered a major decline in both population and industrial growth during the preceding decade) would reap beneficial publicity by serving as the staging ground for the ACLU's test case.

Rappleyea and his associates then prevailed upon a young high-school teacher, John T. Scopes, to serve as the defendant in the trial. Normally, the shy, soft-spoken, twenty-four-year-old Scopes did not even teach biology. But the regular teacher was on sick leave, and Scopes (the school's "general science" instructor and part-time football coach) had temporarily taken over the job. Though far from an intellectual radical, the easygoing Scopes did, in fact, believe in evolution. He agreed to go along with the plan.

In the movie, the fictional town of Hillsboro is represented as a hotbed of religious fantaticism, inhabited by a lynch-mob populace ready to string up anyone heretical enough to question the literal truth of the Bible. The real town of Dayton, by contrast, possessed a very different quality. Even a visitor as profoundly cynical as the acid-tongued journalist H. L. Mencken (the real-life prototype of *Inherit the Wind*'s E. K. Hornbeck) described it as "a country town full of charm and even beauty." Far from having the atmosphere of seventeenth-century Salem at the height of the witch-hunting hysteria, Dayton was pervaded by a genuinely festive air during the trial. As Edward J. Larson describes it in his Pulitzer Prize–winning book, *Summer for the Gods:* "Main Street merchants decorated their shops with pictures of apes and monkeys. One billboard featured a long-tailed primate holding a bottle of patent medicine; another pictured a chimpanzee drinking a soda. The constable's motorcycle carried a sign reading 'Monkeyville Police,' while . . . Robinson's drugstore offered 'simian' sodas." Civic pride (and playfulness) were far more in evidence than rancor, hatred, and bigotry. For the vast majority of Daytonians, persecuting Scopes was not the issue at all. Rather, the townspeople saw themselves as hosting an important event that would attract national interest and attention.

That attention was ensured when William Jennings Bryan announced his intention to enter the case on the side of the prosecution. The model for the fictitious Matthew Brady, Bryan was a far more imposing and admirable figure than the blustering windbag of the movie. An orator of legendary proportions, Bryan—the former secretary of state and three-time Democratic candidate for president—was a political progressive who championed female suffrage, opposed U.S. imperialism, supported laws to control cutthroat corporate practices, and, in many other important ways, applied his prodigious energies to the welfare of the "common man."

He was also an ardent, evangelical Christian who believed in the absolute truth of Scripture and bitterly deplored Darwinism, which he blamed (among other things) for the brutal "survival of the fittest" philosophy that had culminated in the militaristic horrors of World War I. With his tremendous faith in the democratic majority, he also firmly believed, as he once put it, in "the right of the people to have what they want." Since a significant number of Americans—particularly in the south—wanted Darwinian theory banished from their children's classrooms, Bryan felt that Tennessee's antievolution law was fully justified. In short, the principles he came to Dayton to defend were as much social as religious.

Bryan's opponent, the model for the fictional character Henry Drummond, was America's most famous trial lawyer, Clarence Darrow. For Darrow—an avowed agnostic—the issue was simple. He saw the Scopes trial as a chance to do battle against the reactionary forces of Protestant fundamentalism. As he remarked during the proceedings, he had entered the fray for the "purpose of preventing bigots and ignoramuses from controlling the education of the United States."

If *Inherit the Wind* turned Bryan into a far more fatuous figure than he was in real life, it does the opposite with Darrow, portraying him as an American hero of almost Lincolnesque stature. It is certainly true that, from the standpoint of those who believe in intellectual liberty, Darrow fought on the side of the angels. Still, there were many observers of the Scopes trial—and not just fundamentalist fanatics— who were critical of his conduct, particularly during his climactic questioning of Bryan.

That episode—which Edward Larson describes as "the most famous scene in American legal history"—actually took place not inside the cramped, sweltering courtroom but outdoors on the courthouse lawn, on a crudely built platform. Before a rapt audience of more than three thousand people—twice the normal population of the town—Darrow subjected his adversary to what many people regarded as a brutal inquisition. Forced to "choose between his crude beliefs and the common intelligence of modern times" (as Darrow later put it), Bryan ended up looking like a hopeless know-nothing, adamant in his ignorance. "I am more interested in the Rock of Ages than in the ages of rocks," he sputtered at one point when asked about the geologic age of the earth.

But in holding Bryan up to public ridicule, Darrow himself came across, to many people, as a deeply unsympathetic figure—arrogant and mean-spirited. In the movie, even Brady's staunchest supporters desert him at the end, embarrassed by his inane performance on the witness stand. In real life, however, Bryan's followers praised him for "bearing witness bravely to the faith which he believes transcends all the learning of men" (as one newspaper wrote). And when Bryan died in his sleep five days after the trial ended (not, as in the film, while desperately holding forth on the courthouse floor immediately following the verdict), he was hailed as a "martyr who had died defending the Grand Old Fundamental Religion."

In turning the Scopes case into theater, Lawrence and Lee—the original authors of *Inherit the Wind*—paid close attention to historical fact. Very little (beyond the completely fictitious romance between the defendant and the minister's daughter) was invented out of whole cloth. They did, however, simplify the issues, transforming a complex legal case into a black-and-white battle between mindless repression and individual freedom. Clearly, their changes made for more riveting drama. But they had other motives, too. Deeply concerned over the blacklisting of writers and actors, they intended *Inherit the Wind* as a protest over McCarthyism. In short, for all its historical veracity, the play (and movie) had less to do with the events of 1925 than with those of the mid 1950s, when the country faced a far graver threat to its basic intellectual freedom than William Jennings Bryan ever posed.

DARROW FOR THE DEFENSE

Here's a three-part "real-to-reel" trivia question for serious movie buffs:
1. What major motion picture, besides *Inherit the Wind,* featured a character based on the legendary trial lawyer Clarence Darrow?
2. What big Hollywood star (and we use the word "big" advisedly) played this character?
3. What was the character's name?

Answers: 1. *Compulsion.* 2. Orson Welles. 3. Jonathan Wilk.

Jaws

Steven **Spielberg's blockbuster** version of Peter Benchley's bestseller opened in June 1975—just in time to spoil summer vacation for millions of beachgoers, who were so traumatized by the film that they were afraid to go into the water. Set in the fictional town of Amity (located on the east end of Long Island in the novel, though the movie was actually filmed on Martha's Vineyard in Massachusetts), the story concerns a mammoth member of the species *Carcharadon carcharias* (aka the great white shark) that has chosen to turn the waters off the picturesque resort community into his private feeding grounds.

Three men set out to stop the beast—the town's stalwart but aquaphobic police chief, Martin Brody (played by Roy Scheider); a wisecracking ichthyologist named Hooper (Richard Dreyfuss); and a swaggering, foulmouthed charterboat captain named Quint (Robert Shaw). With his colorful (not to say scenery chewing) seafarer shtick, Quint would seem to be a purely fictional creation—a cartoon Captain Ahab whose obsessive hatred of great whites makes Melville's monomaniacal sea captain seem relatively restrained. But in fact, like much about *Jaws*, the character of Quint is firmly rooted in reality—albeit one that the book's creator has never formally acknowledged.

Evidence suggests that the origin of *Jaws* can be traced to a project that got under way in 1968, when legendary diver and documentary filmmaker Peter Gimbel decided to mount a world-ranging expedition to shoot underwater footage of the great white shark, something that had never been accomplished before. Eventually, Gimbel and his intrepid crew found their prey off the coast of South Australia, becoming the first human beings to capture the fearsome sea monster on film. The resulting documentary about their adventure, *Blue Water, White Death*, was released in 1971.

To chronicle his quest, Gimbel invited renowned author-adventurer Peter Matthiessen on the trip. Matthiessen's nonfiction book *Blue Meridian: The Search for the Great White Shark* appeared to great critical acclaim in 1971. And a comparison of *Blue Meridian* to *Jaws* suggests pretty strongly that Benchley was not only familiar with Matthiessen's work but received a fair amount of creative inspiration from it.

Toward the end of *Blue Meridian*, for example, Matthiessen descends into the water in one of Gimbel's patented, aluminum shark cages and describes his first, close-up underwater encounter with a great white:

> *The shark passed slowly, first the slack jaw with the triangular splayed teeth, then the dark eye, impenetrable and empty as*

the eye of God, next the gill slits like knife slashes in paper . . .
Once the smiling head had passed I could reach out and take
hold of the rubber pectoral, or trail my fingers down the length of
the cold dead flank.

Compare this passage to the scene near the end of *Jaws* when
Hooper descends in an aluminum shark cage and has *his* first, close-up
underwater encounter with the great white:

> *The snout passed first, then the jaw, slack and smiling, armed*
> *with row upon row of serrate triangles. And then the black, fath-*
> *omless eye, seemingly riveted upon him. The gills rippled—*
> *bloodless wounds in the steely skin. Tentatively, Hooper stuck a*
> *hand through the bars and touched the flank. It felt cold and*
> *hard, not clammy but smooth as vinyl . . . The fish began to turn,*
> *banking, the rubbery pectoral fins changing pitch.*

The shark cage itself figures prominently in *Jaws* (in one of the
book's most shocking scenes, Hooper is killed when the great white
rams through the bars and chomps him in two; he fares better in the
movie, escaping from the damaged cage and lying low until the monster is destroyed). This apparatus, which was invented by Peter Gimbel, is also discussed at some length by Peter Matthiessen, who
describes the circumstances which led to its creation. "In the summer
of 1960," Matthiessen writes, "Gimbel had come upon a crude old cage
in the backyard of Captain Frank Mundus, whose charter boat, the
Cricket II, sails out of Montauk, New York. Captain Mundus specializes
in sport fishing for sharks, and the cage belonged to a client who was
curious to see what was going on around the baits." As soon as he
glimpsed the clunky steel cage, Gimbel began to envision a more
sophisticated model. By 1965, he had perfected the device.

A year earlier, in June 1964, Captain Mundus had caught a great
white shark off Montauk that meaured seventeen and a half feet in
length and weighed more than four thousand pounds. According to
Matthiessen,

The person most impressed by the Montauk shark was Peter Gimbel . . . In early 1965 he made a pilgrimage to the bar at Salivar's Dock, where the monstrous head resides today in a place of honor on the wall. He stared at the great shark and brooded over it and even dreamed about it, until it became a small kind of obsession. From this time forward, under the sea, he would peer fearfully about him, half expecting the massive shape to materialize in the blue mists. At the same time he longed for the confrontation, if only to exorcise a dread that anyone else would have thought extremely healthy. And in this wish, his film idea was born.

These excerpts from *Blue Meridian* leave little doubt that Peter Benchley received a healthy dose of inspiration from Matthiessen's 1971 book about the exploits, obsessions, and achievements of Peter Gimbel. (Interestingly, the principal photographers of Gimbel's documentary—the husband-wife team of Ron and Valerie Taylor—would eventually shoot the live-action, underwater shark footage for *Jaws*). And Matthiessen's book also offers a clue to the real-life identity of the Ahab-like Quint: the legendary, Long Island fisherman Captain Frank Mundus, who—though never officially acknowledged by Benchley—is widely regarded as the model for the coarse, combative shark hunter of *Jaws*.

A salty, colorful character nicknamed the "Montauk Monster Man," Mundus grew up in Bedford-Stuyvesant and still speaks in heavy Brooklynese. His left arm is scarred and slightly withered—the result, according to local legend, of a savage shark attack. In fact, his injury came from from a severe roller-skating accident he suffered as a nine-year-old boy. After undergoing more than a dozen operations to repair his shattered arm, the doctors recommended salt water, so Frank's father moved the family to the New Jesey shore, where his son could bathe regularly in the ocean. As a result, young Frank's formative years were spent by the sea.

He and his brother went into the fishing business in 1945. Five years later, in June 1951, twenty-six-year-old Frank migrated to Montauk, where a postwar boom in sportfishing was under way. Before long, Mundus had hit on the specialty that would make him a legendary figure—chartering his forty-two-foot boat, the *Cricket II*, for shark-hunting expeditions off the east end of Long Island.

He caught his first great white in 1961, near the little seaside town of Amagansett (the real-life basis, according to Mundus, for Benchley's fictional Amity). Three years later, in June 1964, he caught the 4,500-pound monster whose giant jaws still adorn the wall at Salivar's bar in Montauk. In 1986, he hooked another behemoth, a 3,450-pound great white that he lured with melon chunks and cookies from his perch atop a dead finback whale.

Mundus isn't shy about proclaiming himself the (unacknowledged) "godfather of *Jaws*." Indeed, to hear him tell it, every major incident in the movie and book came directly from his own life. Benchley, Mundus claims, "took his scissors and cut out every article ever written about me. The first scene in the book and movie came from a 3,000-pound white in just 75 feet of water off the bathing beach in Amagansett. There was something in every scene that happened to us right out there. The 4,500-pound white shark was the ending, when we tried to bait a white and had motor trouble. Everything was there, but there was 10 pounds of fiction in every scene. I hate fiction."

Feeling as he does about fiction, Mundus was probably tickled to find himself the star of a critically acclaimed work of nonfiction, journalist Russell Drumm's 1997 book, *In the Slick of the Cricket*.

Jeremiah Johnson

> "Ever chaw on a Sioux liver, Liver-Eatin'?" asked Hatchet Jack.
>
> In wordless answer, Johnson stopped over the Sioux he had just killed. Soon he had the liver in his hands. . . . Holding the trophy for all to see, he sank his teeth into the dripping flesh.
>
> —Raymond Thorpe and Robert Bunker, *Crow Killer*

This **Robert Redford** vehicle concerns a refugee from civilization who (in the words of the theme song) "made his way into the mountains / Bettin' on forgettin' all the troubles that he knew." At the start of the film, the title character arrives in a wilderness outpost, picks up some provisions, and heads off into the Rockies to trap beaver.

At first, he is notably unsuccessful, so inept that he can't even manage to catch a fish or light a fire. Before long, he is reduced to a state of near starvation. Fortunately, he runs into an eccentric but wise old grizzly hunter named Bear Claw Chris Lapp, who instructs him in the ways of the mountain man. After an unspecified period under Bear Claw's tutelage, Jeremiah sets out on his own. Before long, he has picked up a small retinue of companions: a surrogate son (the traumatized child of a massacred white family); a buddy named Del Gue (who shaves his head bald to thwart any Indians with scalping in mind); and a Native American wife (to whom he eventually becomes so devoted that he makes the ultimate sacrifice of shaving off his beard so as not to chafe her face during their lovemaking).

When Jeremiah is coerced into leading a party of soldiers through a sacred Crow burial ground, a band of Crow warriors massacres his wife and "son" in retaliation. From that point on, he becomes a crazed avenger, conducting a one-man guerrilla war against the Crow. Eventually, he gains a reputation as a killer of mythic proportions. The movie ends on a positive note, however, as Jeremiah—facing yet another enemy warrior—thrusts his hand into the air in a gesture of reconciliation. (In a famously perverse bit of interpretation, Pauline Kael, the normally astute film critic for *The New Yorker* magazine, saw things differently: she claimed that Redford was giving the Indian the finger!).

Shot on location out west, the film features truly spectacular wilderness scenery, a number of vivid frontier characters, and colorful backwoods dialect (Del Gue in particular is a highly amusing specimen of the "tall-talking" frontier backwoodsman). Mostly, however, *Jeremiah Johnson* is a paean to those rugged, manly virtues that made our country great: stoic individualism, keeping your mouth shut unless you have something meaningful to say, and good, old-fashioned, relentless frontier violence. That the film is such an unabashed celebration of these red-blooded, all-American values—especially violence—comes as no surprise, since its screenplay was cowritten by John Milius, the two-fisted *auteur* (and proud NRA member) whose credits include *The Wind and the Lion*, *Red Dawn*, and *Conan the Barbarian*. Indeed, if it had been up to Milius, the movie would have been a great deal *more* violent. In the original draft, Johnson not only kills his enemies but devours their livers. Needless to say, these gruesome scenes were eliminated from the final version, since everyone connected with the project (except, apparently, Milius) felt that eating human flesh wasn't entirely consistent with the star's clean-cut image. It *was*, however, consistent with historical truth. The screenplay was based on the life of an actual, flesh-and-blood mountain man whose first name was John, not Jeremiah, and whose proclivity for cannibalism earned him the nickname "Liver-Eating" Johnson.

Virtually everything known about Johnson comes from the oral accounts of people who were acquainted with him—particularly his trapping partner, the real-life Del Gue, and another mountain man named White-Eye Anderson, who, at the age of ninety, shared his recollections with historian Raymond T. Thorpe. Even then—in 1940, when Johnson had been dead for several decades—Anderson was initially reluctant to talk to Thorpe. So fearsome a figure was "The Liver-Eater" that when Thorpe first broached the subject, White-Eye "trembled and turned gray." "Everyone, white and red," he told Thorpe, "had been afraid of Liver-Eating Johnson."

Since nothing (not even his precise date of birth) is known about Johnson's early life, his story (like the movie) begins in the 1840s, when—as a brawny young man of approximately twenty—he stepped off a boat in St. Joseph, Missouri, to commence his career as a fur trapper. Redford's performance in the movie accurately captures the extreme taciturnity of the man, who was strikingly uncommunicative even in a land where actions always spoke louder than words. But in virtually all other respects, the handsome, decent, sensitive frontiersman portrayed by the movie star is a far cry from the real, flesh-and-blood Johnson—a sullen, surly brute of a man with a capacity for violence that bordered on (if it didn't actually cross over into) the sociopathic.

Not long after his arrival out west, Johnson was taken under the wing of a crusty old-timer named John Hatcher, who instructed the youngster in such essential mountain-man skills as beaver trapping, mink skinning, and the most efficient way of scalping a dead Indian. Johnson displayed such an aptitude for this last activity that—after slicing off the topknot of his first slain Arapaho—he received the ultimate accolade from his mentor. "Well, cuss me for a Kiowa!" Hatcher exclaimed. "Ye are better built for this work than any man I ever seed!" Over the years, Johnson would collect hundreds of these grisly trophies (most of which he sold for bounties). But—sentimentalist that he was—he never parted with that very first Indian scalp, keeping it with him until the day he died.

The turning point in Johnson's life occurred just a few years later, when he suddenly developed a craving for female companionship and acquired a Flathead girl from her father for the price of one rifle, a couple of knives, and a few bags of sugar and salt. As in the movie, his bride was named The Swan, apparently because of the unusually graceful curve of her head—her mother having somehow neglected to flatten her infant skull with a rock, according to tribal custom. Back at Johnson's cabin, The Swan faithfully performed her domestic duties, which consisted of all the cooking, cleaning, clothes making, fuel gathering, and packhorse loading, along with about a hundred other menial chores. In return, Johnson expressed his devotion by giving her her own Tennessee rifle and constructing a little corral for her pony.

Their idyllic existence ended abruptly in 1847, when Johnson returned home from a trapping expedition to find a scene of horrible devastation. A party of marauding Crows had murdered and scalped The Swan. Beside her weather-bleached bones lay a second, tiny skeleton—the pathetic remains of a human fetus. The Indians had also pillaged Johnson's cabin, leaving nothing but a copper kettle, which became the burial urn for the bones of his wife and unborn child. Supposedly, it was this tragedy that launched Johnson on his campaign of bloody and cannibalistic revenge.

Within a year, according to historian Thorpe, "news of Johnson's despoiling of the Crows spread through the West. Over a vast territory where white men's campfires were few . . . Crow warriors' bodies—and only Crow warriors' bodies—were found mutilated in special fashion: not merely scalped but cut beneath the ribs and their livers removed." Before long, Johnson had acquired the nicknames by which he would forever be known among Indians and whites: *Dapiek Absakora* ("The

Crow Killer") and Liver-Eating Johnson. A hulking giant of a man with a scraggly red beard and a belt adorned with dried Indian scalps, he caused grown men to step aside in deference and their womenfolk to shudder in dread whenever he appeared in some civilized outpost like Fort Laramie.

After Johnson had dispatched several dozen Crow braves in his trademark style (as Thorpe puts it, "he snapped off the scalps, he carved under the ribs, he ate the dripping liver"), the tribal elders decided to send twenty of their best warriors against him, not in a unified party but individually, each man directed to track down and slay "The Crow Killer" or die trying. They all died trying, defeated in twenty separate bouts of savage hand-to-hand combat. In 1864, Johnson took a break from his vendetta to take part in the Civil War. Even as a Union soldier, however, he couldn't entirely break free of his old habits and ended up killing and scalping a whole slew of Seminole Indians. Though Johnson was severely reprimanded for this behavior and forced to relinquish the scalps, he nevertheless earned an honorable discharge. By the winter of 1865, he was back in the mountains.

Over the next few years, he did his best to maintain his grim reputation. At one time, after taking part in the massacre of thirty-two Sioux Indians, he entertained his buddies by devouring a liver, then superintended as his companions decapitated the corpses, boiled down the skulls, mounted them on poles, and planted them along the riverbank for the benefit of gawking steamboat passengers.

Like his cinematic counterpart, Johnson eventually buried the hatchet with his enemies. In the 1880s, he switched careers, becoming (of all things) a western lawman—first a deputy sheriff, later a marshal. He ended his days in Los Angeles, where he died in the Veterans Hospital on January 21, 1900. He remains, like so many legenday westerners, a deeply ambiguous figure, revered by some as an authentic American hero, regarded by others as a kind of frontier Hannibal Lecter—the bloody-bearded personification of the white man's relentless brutality toward the Indians.

ONE PICTURE IS WORTH $200 MILLION AT THE BOX OFFICE

Certain creators of "real-to-reel" movies get their ideas from newspapers, some from history books, still others from their own personal experiences. The writer-director of one recent blockbuster film was inspired by an unusual source—a single photograph.

The filmmaker in question was Cameron Crowe, who got the brainstorm for his 1997 box-office smash, *Jerry Maguire,* after seeing a photo of former football star Brian "The Boz" Bosworth posing with his agent and friend, Gary Wichard.

At the time the picture was taken, Bosworth—once a swaggering, Mohawked linebacker at the University of Oklahoma—had suffered such extreme setbacks that he entertained serious thoughts of suicide. Having signed an $11 million contract with the Seattle Seahawks, he managed to last only twenty-four games before being forced to quit the profession he loved because of major shoulder problems. Unable to play ball, ride a bike, go to the gym—or even dress himself—without experiencing excruciating pain, Bosworth sank deeper into depression until Wichard helped him get his life back on track by landing the handsome athlete a succession of star-ring roles in fast-paced action movies like *Stone Cold* and *Back in Business.* Eventually, through the help of laser surgery, psychotherapy, a happy mar-riage, and Wichard's support, Bosworth regained his emotional footing. "I'm happier now than ever," he told a reporter in 1997. "Even compared to the height of the Boz, this is the happiest I've ever been."

That newfound happiness was plainly visible in a published photograph showing a beaming Bosworth and a grinning Wichard exchanging an affec-tionate look with each other. As *The New York Times* reported in its issue of January 17, 1997, when filmmaker Cameron Crowe came across the photo, he "was inspired to write a movie about a player and an agent who loved each other."

(continued . . .)

ONE **P**ICTURE **I**S **W**ORTH $200 **M**ILLION AT THE **B**OX **O**FFICE

Of course, to turn his movie into a crowd pleaser, Crowe made one major change. Recognizing that American audiences like nothing better than buddy movies featuring interracial pals (*48 Hours, Lethal Weapon, Men in Black, Die Hard with a Vengeance*, etc.), Crowe transformed the blond, blue-eyed, Nordic-looking Bosworth into the African-American character played so engagingly by Cuba Gooding Jr. (who walked off with a Best Supporting Actor Oscar for the role).

King Kong

Since *King Kong* **is** arguably the greatest fantasy film ever made, it may seem strange to discuss it as an example of a reality-based movie. And we admit that there never was a gigantic, fifty-foot ape who rampaged around Depression-era Manhattan and scaled the Empire State Building with a screeching blonde clutched in one hairy paw. Nevertheless, there really *was* an adventure-packed reality behind the creation of the movie.

That only the most hard-core film buffs can identify the makers of *King Kong* says something significant about the film. Like other pop icons (Superman, Tarzan, Dracula, Sherlock Holmes) Kong seems less the invention of specific individuals than an emanation from our shared, communal dream life—a genuinely mythic figure. But in fact, the movie was the brainchild of two extraordinary men, Merian C. Cooper and Ernest B. Schoedsack, whose amazing true-life adventures inspired the story, and whose personalities are reflected in the figure of *Kong*'s intrepid, globe-trotting filmmaker, Carl Denham.

Cooper and Schoedsack originally met during the waning days of World War I when the two adventurous young men found themselves in Poland, helping in the fight against the Bolsheviks. Though only in his twenties, Cooper in particular had already led an unusually eventful life. After serving in the Georgia National Guard during the Pancho Villa campaign, he had joined the Aviation Corps during the Great War and served on the western front, flying reconnaissance missions over Germany. Shot down and captured by the enemy, he spent a month in a military hospital before being freed after the armistice.

Joining forces with the Polish army as part of a ten-man American squadron, Cooper flew seventy strafing missions over Bolshevik lines. In July 1919, he was forced to make a landing when his plane was disabled by ground fire. Captured by Cossack horsemen, he was taken prisoner by the Red Army, transported to Moscow, and put to work in a labor camp.

In April 1921, Cooper made a daredevil escape. After nearly three harrowing weeks of travel, he made his way back to Warsaw, where he was greeted as a hero. Shortly afterward he again encountered Schoedsack, a movie cameraman who had served with the Army Signal Corps. The two young men talked about collaborating one day on a film set in some exotic locale. In the meantime, Cooper sailed back to New York City, where he became a writer for *The New York Times*. Schoedsack headed for the Aegean port of Smyrna, where he participated in the Greco-Turkish War of 1921–22, eventually winning a Distinguished Service Cross for his bravery.

Their first opportunity to work together came in 1922, when Cooper was hired by a globe-trotting adventurer, Captain Edwin Salisbury, who planned to sail around the world, producing documentary films, travel books, and magazine articles, about far-flung places. When the original cameraman quit, Schoedsack was brought on board. Over the following months, the three men—along with a hybrid crew of Americans, Danes, Samoans, and a colorful Ceylonese cook nicknamed "Shamrock"—had a string of adventures, encountering pygmies, surviving a monsoon, escaping Arab marauders, shooting the first movies ever made of the pilgrims to Mecca. Unfortunately, all the footage was destroyed when the ship went up in flames while dry-docked in Italy.

By then, Cooper and Schoedsack had already come up with the concept for another movie—a documentary on the order of Robert Flaherty's pioneering *Nanook of the North*, depicting man's struggle to survive in a harsh, natural environment. Their idea was to travel to Turkey and film the migratory movements of a local nomadic tribe. Traveling back to New York City to seek financing, Cooper contacted a friend named Marguerite Harrison, an extraordinary young widow who had led a life every bit as adventurous as his own.

An accomplished newspaper reporter and travel writer, Harrison had gone to Europe after World War I, where—under the pretext of her journalistic investigations—she had collected information for the American intelligence service. She had first encountered Cooper at a ball in Warsaw while on her way to an assignment in the U.S.S.R. When Cooper was later imprisoned in Moscow, she had smuggled him food, money, and tobacco—until her own arrest on an espionage charge. Eventually, Harrison was released and deported back to the U.S., where she was hailed by the press as the only woman ever imprisoned by the Soviets as a spy.

With Harrison along as a partner in the venture, Cooper returned to Paris and reunited with Schoedsack. The adventurous trio then made their way to Persia, where they learned about a nomadic people called the Bakhtiari, who made an arduous trek every winter across an awesome mountain range in search of grazing lands for their cattle. For forty-six days, the three intrepid filmmakers accompanied the tribe on this hazardous journey, becoming the first foreigners ever to cross the snow-buried Zardeh Kuh mountain.

The documentary film that resulted from this expedition, *Grass*, opened to critical acclaim in 1925 and immediately attracted the interest of Jesse Lasky, one of Hollywood's pioneering film moguls. When Lasky agreed to subsidize another Cooper-Schoedsack project, the pair immediately set out for the tropical jungles of Siam. There—in a region so remote that no white hunter had ever penetrated it—they found a native population that, for years, had been terrorized by man-eating jungle cats. Exposing themselves to tremendous peril, the two film-makers shot footage of rampaging tigers, stampeding elephants, slithering pythons, and other exotic creatures.

Back in the United States, the footage was assembled into a thrilling documentary called *Chang*, which proved to be an enormous success upon its release in 1927. With his profits from the film, Cooper invested in the budding civil aviation industry, becoming so successful that, before long, he found himself on the executive boards of several airlines, including Pan Am. While his partner headed off to Sumatra to shoot another movie, Cooper now found himself stuck in a New York City office building. Seated behind his desk, he continued to daydream of dangerous, unexplored lands. One dream in particular kept coming back to haunt him: a fantasy of a mysterious, skull-shaped island in the Malay waters, where the savage tribesman worship a living jungle god, a fifty-foot-tall, prehistoric ape.

Eventually Cooper—teamed up again with his old partner, Schoedsack—got a chance to transform that fantasy into *King Kong*, a film that is suffused with the true-life experiences of its remarkable creators. The brash, globe-trotting filmmaker Carl Denham, celebrated for his thrilling "animal pictures," is a composite of Cooper and Schoedsack. Ann Darrow, the spunky woman who becomes the giant beast's unwilling love object, is partly based on Marguerite Harrison. And the exotic adventures recorded in *Chang* became the prototype for the jungle thrills and perils that Denham and his companions encounter in *King Kong*. (Indeed, the name "Kong" itself appears to have been derived from the similar-sounding "Chang"—a Lao word that, in the context of the film, signifies a mysterious jungle beast that strikes fear into the hearts of the natives.)

Eventually, Cooper and Schoedsack found it so hard to separate their real lives from the fantasy world of *King Kong* that, in the end, they felt compelled to step inside the movie. "We should kill the son of a bitch ourselves," Cooper reportedly told Schoedsack. And that's just what they did. In the film's famous climactic sequence, where navy biplanes shoot Kong down from the Empire State Building, the two men can be seen in the roles of the pilot and gunner, who deliver the *coup de grâce* to the doomed, love-struck monster.

The Last Hurrah

For better or worse, they just don't make politicians like they used to. Spencer Tracy, as Boston mayor Frank Skeffington in *The Last Hurrah*, embodies this idea as well as any other character in American movies. He is a leader with the common touch, who receives a line of needy constituents each day and attempts to handle whatever personal problems they bring his way. He is also an unabashed finagler and a silver-tongued devil, full of adroit Irish blarney, ready to turn a wake into a political caucus and willing to stoop to blackmail to accomplish his aims. Based on Edwin O'Connor's bestselling novel and directed by John Ford, the master of Irish Americana on film, *The Last Hurrah* is gently nostalgic for this kind of public servant, for all his faults. And not just for this *type* of public servant. The movie taps into the legacy of one Boston politician in particular.

James Michael Curley looms large in Boston history as one of the city's most active officeholders, a man responsible for building much of modern Beantown's infrastructure and public works. At the same time, he was fabulously corrupt. There were few methods of subterfuge or arm-twisting that he would not resort to. And no matter how brazen he became, he always managed to ride high in the eyes of his supporters.

In fact, it seemed that the *more* brazen he got, the more popular he became. No disgrace could stop him. Once he even succeeded in getting elected while serving time in prison.

Like Frank Skeffington, James Curley grew up in Boston's slums and spent his career combating Boston blue-bloods for the sake of his Irish working-class brethren. (In another parallel between film and fact, William O'Connell, also an Irish son of the Boston tenements, grew up to become a cardinal and an opponent of Curley, as is the case with the Donald Crisp character in *The Last Hurrah*.) At an early age, Curley decided to devote himself to a political life. He won his first election, as a Boston common-council member, at the age of twenty-six. His talents for rousing oratory and backroom maneuvering led to a succession of other victories at the polls and a variety of public offices. By the time he was thirty-six, he had served as an alderman, a state legislator, a city councilman, and a U.S. congressman.

It was while running for alderman that he spent the first of his two terms in prison.

Curley based much of his success on creating the impression that he would do anything for his supporters. In 1903, one of his ward workers was angling for a postal job, but it was clear that his ambition outstripped his aptitude even for this fairly prosaic goal. He needed assistance in passing the civil service exam, and so Curley, always eager to help those who could help him, took the exam for him. Subsequently convicted of fraud, alderman-candidate Curley was sentenced to ninety days in jail. Not only did his prison stretch fail to spoil his election hopes, it would remain a source of pride for him in years to come. When Curley would address a crowd, one of his confederates would often rise on cue and demand that the speaker explain his stint in jail. The reply was simple, and invariably it elicited approval. "I did it for a friend," Curley would say.

The Last Hurrah may make it clear that its protagonist is willing to indulge in unorthodox tactics, but Frank Skeffington's methods pale in comparison to Curley's way of getting things done, especially at election time. A favorite ploy of his was to raise the specter of the Ku Klux Klan, which was enjoying a resurgence at the time and whose antipapistry presented an unsettling threat to Curley's predominently Irish-Catholic constituents. Once while running for mayor, Curley paid a local Klanner $2,000 to endorse his opponent. During a gubernatorial race, he went a step further. Whenever he stumped before a crowd outside the city, a cross would suddenly burst into flames on a nearby hillside, providing Curley the dramatic opportunity to expound upon the Klan menace. Setting the stage, of course, were hired cross burners who followed Curley wherever he went.

At times, Curley's machinations seemed almost magical. In 1932, he was dead set on attending the Democratic National Convention in order to press for Franklin Roosevelt's nomination. But political enemies at home barred him from the Massachusetts delegation, supposedly leaving him out in the cold. Somehow, though, Curley wangled his way into the delegation from, of all places, Puerto Rico, and succeeded in announcing the territory's support for FDR under the guise of "Don Jaime Miguel Curleo."

Although he held many offices, Curley was best known for his four terms as mayor of Boston. He was responsible for the repaving of roads, the expansion of public transportation, and the construction of playgrounds and hospitals, all of which also put many unemployed people to work. To accomplish all this, Curley emptied the city treasury more than once. At one time, funds were so low that the government couldn't even afford to pay its employees. Whenever he was faced with this sort of fiscal crisis, Curley found some way to secure a loan. Sometimes, though—as is dramatized in *The Last Hurrah*—the banks were not cooperative. At least not at first. In one case, Curley threatened to instigate a run on a bank if it did not come across. In another instance, he suggested that the plumbing beneath a bank might just accidentally flood if he did not see a more civic-minded attitude on the bank officials' part.

No matter what Curley did, his political career continued onward. In 1947, two months after winning his fourth mayoral election, he was convicted on a charge of mail fraud for his involvement with a shady wartime contractor several years earlier. Once again, he was sentenced to prison, this time for five months. Upon his release, he resumed his duties as mayor and the public welcomed him back, completely unfazed by his latest excursion behind bars.

Edwin O'Connor's novel *The Last Hurrah* was published in 1956, a year after Curley's last campaign for mayor, which he lost. At first, Curley was outraged by the book and threatened to sue. In time, though, he came to see the novel as good publicity, since Skeffington was a sympathetic portrait. Eventually, in jocular moments, he would even use the Skeffington moniker when signing his name.

Jim Curley died on November 12, 1958, shortly after Spencer Tracy first appeared on movie screens as the political boss's fictionalized incarnation. While Tracy drew viewers into theaters, Curley pulled in a crowd of 100,000 Boston citizens as he lay in state.

The Last of the Mohicans

Few fictional characters have been as influential as Hawkeye, the hero of this 1992 version of James Fenimore Cooper's classic adventure novel. Also known as Leatherstocking and Natty Bumppo, he was originally created in 1823 and appeared in five Cooper novels in all. A sharpshooting loner of the wilderness, he has served as the model for hundreds of frontier swashbucklers both in print and on film. It is only fitting that such an archetypal fictional hero should have been modeled, in turn, upon America's prototypical real-life frontier hero.

Daniel Boone died just three years before Cooper first wrote about his buckskin protagonist. His genuine exploits were already legendary, ever since they had first been popularized in a ghostwritten autobiography in 1784. Like Hawkeye, Boone was a crack shot and an accomplished woodsman who played a key role in spearheading westward expansion. Beginning at the age of sixteen, he spent his early adulthood on so-called long hunts, months-long excursions into the wilderness to collect valuable hides and furs. Based on his knowledge of the area, he was hired by land speculators to lead settlers into the Kentucky forests. Here he gained fame as an Indian fighter and as a pathfinder who helped blaze the Wilderness Road that opened the region to settlement. In later years, he continued his westward wandering by venturing with his family to Missouri, where he eventually died in 1820.

In addition to their abilities and reputations, Boone and Hawkeye share another important trait: their attitudes toward white men and Native Americans. In the opening scenes of *The Last of the Mohicans*, there is a memorable image of Hawkeye (played by Daniel Day-Lewis) scrambling pantherlike through the forest. Except for skin color, there appears to be no significant difference between him and his Indian companions, Chingachcook and Uncas. The same sort of affinity with Native Americans could be found in Boone's life. He may not have qualified as a Day-Lewis-style hunk, and he may not have enacted his adventures in the close company of Indian blood brothers, but while on his long hunts, he lived much the same as a Native American woodsman. In fact, many European settlers regarded him as, in effect, a white Indian. He helped bring white settlements to the wilderness, but he was not comfortable with European-American civilization and spent much of his life moving westward away from its influence. He fought Indians in many skirmishes along the frontier, but he had many friends among the Cherokees and the Shawnees and would often hunt with them. At one point, while a captive of the Shawnees, he was adopted into the tribe. Like Hawkeye, he was a man caught between two worlds.

Of all of Cooper's Leatherstocking Tales, *The Last of the Mohicans* has an especially close connection to Daniel Boone lore. Not only is its hero modeled after the real-life frontiersman, its principal plot thread—the hero's rescue of a woman kidnapped by Indians—was inspired by a famous episode from Boone's life.

In 1776, the renowned trailblazer and his family were living in the namesake Kentucky settlement of Boonesborough. On a Sunday afternoon in July, Boone's thirteen-year-old daughter, Jemima, left the fortified community to go canoeing on the Kentucky River with two teenage friends, Fanny and Betsy Callaway. Spying them from the riverbank brush was a war party of two Cherokees and three Shawnees, who had recently killed an isolated homesteader. They pulled the canoe to the shore opposite the settlement. The girls screamed for help but were soon silenced when the Indian raiders threatened them with their knives. The Cherokees and Shawnees marched the girls into the woods.

The screams woke Boone from an afternoon nap. He raced barefoot to the river and quickly took command of the rescue party that congregated there. Crossing the river, they plunged into the forest and took up the kidnappers' trail. They were still far behind the raiding party when they made camp at nightfall. Boone sent a messenger back to Boonesborough to bring back weapons and supplies for what promised to be an arduous chase.

The kidnapped girls did their part to slow their captors down. Jemima Boone exaggerated a foot injury and limped along as slowly as she could. She and her companions also left sign at every opportunity, breaking branches and pulling up vines.

The next morning, Boone made the first of two fateful decisions that would ultimately allow him to overtake the Indians. Searching the woods for sign, he knew, made his progress torturously slow. He decided instead to leave the trail behind and head directly northward. He had surmised that the raiders were headed for Indian towns in that direction. His judgment proved correct. Later in the day, the rescue party came across markings left behind by the girls. The next day, Boone gained some more ground by leaving the trail once again and striking out on a course that he believed would intercept the kidnappers' trail. By afternoon, the search party came across the carcass of a freshly butchered buffalo. They were very close now.

In a glen up ahead, the Cherokee/Shawnee party stopped to roast the buffalo meat. They joked easily, seemingly confident that they had lost their pursuers. Jemima Boone and her two friends huddled together. Their last shreds of hope had evaporated. Then Jemima heard something. She looked up at a ridge and saw her father, crawling silently along the ground like a snake. He motioned her to remain quiet and still as he and the other rescuers took their positions surrounding the camp. One of Boone's comrades, unable to hold back any longer, opened fire.

The shot punched through the torso of one of the Indians. In a moment, a full volley of gunfire rained down, and another kidnapper was mortally wounded. In the excitement, Betsy Callaway jumped to her feet. A nearby Indian swung his war club, which brushed past her head. But before he could take another swing, the rescuers charged down the slope. Surprised and outnumbered, the rest of the Cherokees and Shawnees fled into the woods. They made no attempt to strike back.

It would take the imagination of James Fenimore Cooper to elaborate this episode into an early American epic. And it would take the artfulness of director Michael Mann to fashion Cooper's tale of captivity and rescue into a compelling, moving adventure film. But for Boone and his companions, the actual, unadorned experience would be more than cathartic enough. Once the surviving kidnappers had scattered, Boone's party and the rescued girls all gathered together and began to cry from relief. According to Jemima Boone, "There was not a dry eye in the company."

Looking for Mr. Goodbar

An unpleasantly puritanical air pervades this 1977 adaptation of Judith Rossner's runaway bestseller. Essentially, it is a finger-wagging, tongue-clucking attack on the excesses of the freewheeling, pre-AIDS 1970s, when—according to the vision of screenwriter-director Richard Brooks—homicidal gays ran rampant on the streets of New York City and every block featured a swinging-singles bar patronized by predatory studs and lonely young women cruising for casual pick-ups.

Diane Keaton stars as Theresa Dunn, one of the more winsome of these desperate, doomed females. Brought up in a repressive Irish-Catholic household, Theresa suffers from a deep-seated sense of insecurity, having been afflicted with scoliosis (curvature of the spine) as a child. Though smart, beautiful, and totally dedicated to the deaf students she teaches at her day job, Theresa is hopelessly screwed up when it comes to her personal relationships. She despises the handsome, idealistic, "nice young man" who pursues her (William Atherton).

Sweetness and devotion leave her cold; what really turns her on is humiliation and mistreatment, which she receives in abundance from her many sex partners. After a long-term affair with her insufferable, married college professor, she plunges ever more deeply into a life of sordid one-night stands with a string of increasingly questionable characters (the most memorable of whom is the insanely narcissistic street tough played by Richard Gere in his first major role). In the end, Theresa picks up one stranger too many—a sexually confused former convict (effectively portrayed by a young and Brando-esque Tom Berenger), who ends up proving his masculinity by savagely murdering her in the film's powerfully unsettling climax.

In creating the fictional Theresa Dunn—her innermost fantasies, feelings, desires, motivations, etc.—Judith Rossner relied primarily on her own imagination. But the basic story of *Looking for Mr. Goodbar* was inspired by a shocking true-life crime, the brutal 1973 murder of a twenty-seven-year-old New York City schoolteacher named Katherine Cleary.

Like her fictional counterpart, Cleary—the oldest of three children of devout Irish-Catholic parents—developed scoliosis as a child. At ten, she had a spinal operation and spent a solid year recuperating. The procedure helped straighten out her crooked shoulders but left her with a pronounced limp, an eleven-inch scar on her back, and a profound sense of physical insecurity, alienation, and self-contempt.

Rebelling against the conservative values of her parents—who expected her to fulfill the traditional roles of housewife and mother—Katherine left home at eighteen, enrolled in a state teachers college, became involved in the 1960s civil rights movement, and started dating African-American men. Eventually, she moved to an apartment in Manhattan. By day, she tended to live a quiet, sedate life as a teacher (first in the public schools of Newark, later at St. Joseph's School for the Deaf in the Bronx). At night, however, the petite, freckle-faced redhead turned into a boisterous, sexually promiscuous party girl, picking up disreputable-looking strangers at neighborhood bars and taking them home for bouts of rough sex.

One of those strangers—the last she would ever pick up—was a young man named Joe Willie Simpson. Born in small-town Illinois, Joe Willie had been raised by grim, midwestern parents who (according to one social worker) might have served as the models for Grant Wood's famous painting, *American Gothic*. A chronic runaway with a long history of psychiatric problems, he'd been in and out of mental institutions from the time he was twelve. At sixteen—blond, blue-eyed, muscular—he hitchhiked around the country, eventually ending up in Times Square, where he took to petty thievery and homosexual hustling.

In the summer of 1970, a thirty-nine-year-old man named Danny Murray—cruising Times Square for sex—spotted the twenty-year-old hustler. Before long, Joe Willie was ensconced in Murray's penthouse apartment. The young drifter's life during the next two years was characteristically erratic. After stealing some cash and credit cards from his sugar daddy, he headed down to Miami, where he met and married a sixteen-year-old girl named Carole Musty, got arrested for robbery, and broke out of jail after serving a few months of his one-year sentence.

Returning to New York City, Joe Willie and his teenage bride settled into the apartment of the all-forgiving Murray. Determined to be a breadwinner for his wife, Joe Willie hit the streets and started hustling again. When Carole got pregant, he made a stab at normality, taking a job as a mail clerk. But respectability wasn't Joe Willie's long suit, and before long, he was back to his old ways.

Late on New Year's Day 1973, both Katherine Cleary and Joe Willie Simpson ended up at an Upper West Side bar called Tweed's. Precisely what happened between them will never be known. From later reconstructions (such as the one pieced together by journalist Lacey Fosburgh in her book *Closing Time: The True Story of the "Goodbar" Murder*), it appears that—after sharing a few drinks and some small talk with the good-looking young stranger—Katherine took him back to her cramped, unkempt apartment a few doors down the block. According to the account Joe Willie later gave to police, the two of them had sex. Immediately afterward Katherine (who appears to have had a masochistic streak and liked to taunt her pickups into roughing her up) "got real nasty," pushing and shoving Joe Willie and telling him to leave. Joe Willie—unstable in the best of circumstances—"flipped out" and savagely attacked her, choking her with his bare hands, strangling her with her panties, stabbing her with a paring knife, stuffing a candle up her vagina, smashing her face with a statuette, and chewing fiercely on her breasts.

After cleaning himself off in the shower, he returned home and confessed to Murray, who gave him plane fare and shipped him off to Miami. Two days later, Katherine Cleary's savaged body was found by a coworker, concerned about her absence from school. The brutal killing of the young schoolteacher was headline news. A panicky Murray—suddenly afraid that he would be charged as an accomplice—told police about Joe Willie, who was promptly arrested and returned to New York City, where he was jailed in the Tombs. Five months later, shortly after noon on May 5, 1973, he tossed a sheet over a ceiling bar in his cell and hanged himself. Danny Murray claimed the body and personally escorted it back to Illinois for burial. On the very day of the funeral, Joe Willie's young wife, Carole, gave birth to a stillborn baby—an eerily fitting end to a sordid, sensational case that produced nothing but heartbreak and death.

M

In the early 1930s, serial-killer thrillers were a rarity. In fact, the term "serial murder" would not even be coined until some forty years later. But the great German director Fritz Lang was a cinematic pioneer, and in the 1931 film *M*, he tackled the nearly unprecedented themes of sexual obsession and homicidal mania. He cast a young Peter Lorre as Hans Beckert, one of the most unsettling fictional murderers ever created, a man driven by twisted passions to strangle small children. When devising this character, Lang did not have to use a great deal of imagination.

Serial murder may be a type of crime that is most often associated with the contemporary American scene, but to one degree or another, it has been with us throughout history. Germany after World War I was a particularly fertile breeding ground for this terrifying strain of homicide. Killers with a cannibalistic streak were particularly prominent. In Hanover, Fritz Haarmann murdered around fifty boys and devoured some of their flesh, selling the rest on the street to customers who believed they were buying beef or pork. In Berlin, Georg Grossmann also peddled human flesh, carved from the bodies of murdered women, while in Muensterburg, Karl Denke butchered at least eight men for his own personal consumption. When Lang and his collaborator, Thea von Harbou, were preparing their *M* script in Berlin, a savage killer named Peter Kurten awaited trial in a jail cell at the other end of Germany. The crimes of Lang's child strangler were patterned upon the atrocities committed by Kurten, who was known throughout the country at the time as the Monster of Düsseldorf.

This real-life bogeyman was born in 1883. His life was horrific from the very beginning. He and his ten siblings, crammed into a single-room flat, lived at the mercy of an alcoholic, sex-offender father, or at least they did until 1897, when the courts sent the Kurten patriarch to prison for attempting to rape one of his daughters. Truly his father's son, Peter Kurten would occasionally molest his sisters himself. Whatever depravity he didn't inherit from his father he gleaned from a neighbor, a sort of role model for Kurten, who taught the boy how to sexually violate and torture dogs.

Kurten may have committed his first murder at the age of nine. According to his later confession, he was out rafting with two other boys at the time and he drowned both of them in such a way as to make the killings look like an accident. This crime has never been confirmed. Perhaps Kurten fabricated the story to burnish his reputation as a senseless murderer, a reputation that he took great pride in. Whatever the truth of the matter, he would spend the next thirty-seven years stoking his deranged passions until they finally exploded into a rampage of murder and terror. In those thirty-seven years, he committed arson, burglary, and sexual assault, and served as much time in prison as out. Then, in Düsseldorf between February 1929 and May 1930, he murdered at least thirteen people and wounded many others.

In *M*, the Peter Lorre character preys on one type of victim (children) and restricts himself to one, almost ritualistic method of murder (strangulation). In this regard, Lang exercised artistic license, not in embroidering the truth but in narrowing the scope of it. Kurten did, in fact, murder children, and he was fond of choking his victims, but his mania was much wider ranging. He killed men, women, and children, and attacked them with his bare hands as well with hammer, scissors, knife, and ax. No doubt, director Fritz Lang decided he had to zero in on one type of Kurten murder for the sake of dramatic focus.

As varied as his methods may have been, there was one obsession that connected all of Kurten's crimes—the unnervingly close association of violence and sex. Often he would strangle women while raping them to accentuate his arousal. Stabbing or bludgeoning his victims could produce the same kind of twisted fervor. One of his most famous crimes actually was not a murder, since it did not involve a human being. One night, while strolling through a park, he came upon a swan asleep by a lake. Overcome by one of his grotesque impulses, he immediately grabbed the bird. "I cut its throat," he later said. "The blood spurted up and I drank from the stump and ejaculated." He would also drink the blood from wounds in the temple or throat of some of his human victims.

Given the unspeakable nature of Kurten's murder spree, it should come as no surprise that he provoked a panic throughout Düsseldorf that was easily equal to the panic portrayed in *M*. One horribly ravaged body after another was discovered, and for a year the police could not pick up the killer's trail. They interrogated approximately nine thousand people and sifted through some two hundred crank confessions and ultimately called on the services of psychics to help steer them in the right direction. One of the investigation's stumbling blocks was the police's astonishment at the extent of the crimes. They found it hard to believe that only one man could be responsible.

The only legitimate leads came, as they did in Lang's film, from the killer himself. Unable to suppress his bloodthirsty pride, he felt compelled to write an anonymous letter to a newspaper boasting of his latest atrocity, the murder of a five-year-old girl whom he had strangled, stabbed thirty-six times, then set ablaze. To make sure that his handiwork would be discovered, Kurten enclosed a map of the area where the murder occurred.

One other similarity between the Lang film and the actual case was the outrage expressed by the conventional criminal underworld. Düsseldorf hoodlums were so frequently harassed by the police during the search for the monstrous serial murderer that they took it upon themselves to scour the city for the killer themselves. In *M*, it is ultimately this sort of manhunt, by thieves, beggars, and gangsters that traps the child strangler. The underworld even drags Hans Beckert before an ad hoc tribunal. In real life, however, it was the killer himself who was most responsible for the conclusion to the case. Acting like someone who wanted to be caught, Kurten abducted a woman in May 1930 and attempted to rape her in a lonely stretch of woods, but then allowed her to get away. When the woman told her story to the police, the authorities finally had a witness who could lead them to the culprit.

Upon Kurten's arrest, the police discovered another reason the murderer had been able to escape capture for so long. The so-called Monster of Düsseldorf did not look like a monster at all. He looked like a smartly dressed, middle-class clerk. Only by gazing deeply into his cold, empty eyes could one possibly guess at the true deranged nature of the man. And the only people who were likely to have done that were his victims—who usually did not live to tell any tales—and his wife of ten years, who, incredibly enough, never knew anything about his secret life.

In the mesmerizing final scene of *M*, Peter Lorre, as the killer, delivers a speech to the underworld tribunal, attempting to explain the bizarre impulses that lay behind his unforgivable crimes. Managing to get across both the anguish and the ferocity of the character, Lorre comes close to making us sympathize with this monster. Peter Kurten, on the other hand, did not elicit much sympathy from anybody, as he freely confessed his crimes with obvious relish. At the end of his trial, the jury needed only ninety minutes to deliver a guilty verdict on nine counts of murder. At one point, Kurten made an attempt, as so many serial killers do, to cop an insanity plea. In the end, though, he probably was not too disappointed that this ploy had failed. There was something about being executed, after all, that intrigued him. Before he was guillotined on July 2, 1931, he said that he eagerly anticipated the experience of hearing the blood gush from his own severed neck stump.

The Man Who Came to Dinner

> "I'm not always that rude and I'm not always that funny. What the boys have done is bring out the worst and best of me."
>
> —Alexander Woollcott, on the Sheridan Whiteside character in George S. Kaufman and Moss Hart's play *The Man Who Came to Dinner*

In 1938, George S. Kaufman and Moss Hart promised they would write a play for a friend of theirs. The friend was the well-known critic, radio personality, and occasional actor Alexander Woollcott. The play was to be a starring vehicle for him. When Kaufman and Hart finally wrote the piece a year later, they decided that the only character worthy of Woollcott would be Woollcott himself. No other fictional creation would have been sufficiently quirky, maddening, or entertaining.

Alexander Woollcott was considered to be one of the wittiest people of his day. Also one of the most incorrigible. He presided as a leading light of the famed Algonquin Round Table, the circle of sharp-tongued writers and actors that included Robert Benchley, Dorothy Parker, and the Marx Brothers. He reached millions of readers and listeners with his reviews and commentaries, and he was friend to many of the most famous people of the twenties and thirties. The Kaufman/Hart creation known as Sheridan Whiteside, the title character in *The Man Who Came to Dinner*, was every bit as caustic, petty, tyrannical, and conniving as Woollcott was. Woollcott was quite pleased with the character. Ultimately, though, he declined to play the role.

He thought it would be unseemly of him to exploit his persona so openly. More to the point, he was nervous about putting himself on the spot. Not only would the public and the critics pass judgment on his performance but on his personality as well. The role went instead to Monty Woolley, who scored a huge success on Broadway with the Kaufman/Hart play and went on to star in 1941 film version as well. Once he saw how eagerly people received the play, Woollcott portrayed the character himself in a road company production. His performance came just five years before he died and would serve as a fitting, outrageous climax to a colorful career.

Born in 1887, the precocious young Woollcott secured his first newspaper assignments while still in high school when he wrote book reviews for the *Philadelphia Telegraph*. A few years later, at Hamilton College, the owlish, corpulent Woollcott began to shape his persona, a mixture of brilliance and eccentricity. While earning various academic honors, he would amble across campus in baggy corduroy pants, turtleneck sweater, and a red fez with gilt tassel.

After graduation he landed a job at *The New York Times*, where he worked his way up from gofer to reporter, a job for which he was not particularly well suited. As one observer put it, he was "not exactly hostile to facts, but apathetic about them." He found his true calling when he switched to theater reviewing.

As a critic, he knew no middle ground. He would either wax rhapsodic or seethe with venom. Either way, his writing was always vivid, and soon he emerged as the premier theater critic in New York. He upheld that reputation as he moved on to the *New York Herald* and

New York Sun, then broadened his range of extreme opinions as a magazine-feature writer, radio commentator, and lecturer.

When he wasn't holding forth at the Algonquin, he was holding court at his apartment, where many of the celebrities of the era came to see him. Often, whether they planned on it or not, they came to be insulted by him. His charm, when he decided to turn it on, must have been impressive, because it was enough to overshadow his other qualities. He was fond of greeting his friends with, "Hello, repulsive," and then later sending them on their way with, "I find you are beginning to disgust me. How about getting the hell out of here?" At times, he could make comments at his own expense, as he once did at a party for English author Rebecca West. After dropping to his knees and embracing West, Woollcott, the lifelong bachelor, said, "That is my sex life for 1933." But it would be Woollcott at his most difficult that provided the creative spark for *The Man Who Came to Dinner*.

When Hart and Kaufman promised to write a play for him, Woollcott had already appeared in two productions by S. M. Behrman. As an actor, he was more of an entertaining amateur than a professional, but audiences clearly responded to his acerbic manner. According to Malcolm Goldstein's biography of Kaufman, Hart developed the concept for the play when he had the dubious pleasure of taking on Woollcott as an overnight houseguest. Woollcott was in rare form. He commandeered Hart's bedroom, accused Hart's servants of dishonesty, and wound things up by writing in his host's guest book, "I wish to say that on my first visit to Moss Hart's house I had one of the most unpleasant evenings I can ever recall having spent." The next time Hart met with Kaufman, he came up with a chilling conjecture: what if Woollcott had descended upon his house and then had broken his leg and had to stay? Beginning with this desperate premise, the playwrights devised a hilarious, barb-tongued comedy.

The story opens with Sheridan Whiteside—Woollcott in fictional guise—barnstorming across the midwest on a lecture tour, making a stop in the provincial Ohio town of Mesalia. When visiting the home of a local ball-bearings manufacturer for dinner, he slips on the house's icy steps and breaks his hip. Under doctor's orders, he remains in the house and turns it into his personal domain. He uses the threat of a lawsuit to banish the family to the outer reaches of the house while he takes over the entire first floor. When not verbally abusing the family, he meddles in their lives (another Woollcott trait) and entertains a steady stream of guests, ranging from theatrical stars to convicted murderers and penguins.

A true comedy *à clef*, *The Man Who Came to Dinner* features several recognizable personalities in addition to Woollcott/Whiteside. Lorraine Sheldon (Ann Sheridan), the vampish Broadway star, is a send-up of Gertrude Lawrence; Beverly Carlton (Reginald Gardiner), the witty, self-absorbed playwright is a thinly disguised Noël Coward; and Banjo (Jimmy Durante), the wild, girl-chasing comic, is clearly based on Harpo Marx (although the movie version makes the connection just slightly less obvious by deleting the play's references to Banjo's brothers, Wacko and Sloppo).

Woollcott was deeply gratified by the success of the play and film, even if he couldn't resist taking a facetious swipe at it. "Of course this is a libelous caricature," he said. "It is not true that the role of the obnoxious Sheridan Whiteside . . . was patterned after me. Whiteside is merely a composite of the better qualities of the play's two authors."

A wry coda to the story: Kaufman and Hart were subjected to a frivolous lawsuit by a would-be playwright who claimed that they had plagiarized his work. "It seems we stole the character of Woollcott from the play *Sticks and Stones*," Kaufman wrote to the real Sheridan Whiteside. "It will probably turn out that you got it from there, too."

Matinee

In this period piece set in 1962, John Goodman stars as Lawrence Woolsey, a flamboyantly seedy movie producer. To many, his machinations might seem patently preposterous. He promotes his latest low-grade horror film by boasting of its revolutionary new motion-picture processes entitled "Atomovision" and "Rumblerama." These purported technological "miracles" involve buzzing theater seats, smoke bombs ignited in front of the screen, a guy dressed in a rubber ant costume who runs amuck through the audience, and a simulated atomic fireball that bursts through the movie screen directly at the viewers, triggering a mad rush for the exits. Clearly a bunch of juvenile nonsense, as far as sensible, mature filmgoers are concerned. But those in the know— especially those who know their horror movies from the late fifties and early sixties—are aware that all of this is based on fact. The shameless ballyhoo of Lawrence Woolsey was clearly modeled after the promotional antics of schlockmeister William Castle.

From 1958 to 1961, Castle produced and directed a series of six movies that set new standards for publicity-mad gimmickry. With such low-budget shockers as *The Tingler* and *House on Haunted Hill*, he could be counted on to promise more thrills than he could possibly deliver and to conjure up spectacular film "processes" that always proved to be considerably less than spectacular. He was Hollywood's premier flim-flam showman, but he also made movie watching a unique, rambunctious experience for baby-boom horror aficionados.

Castle actually made movies for fifteen years before finally emerging as the great schlock icon of his day. During that time, he directed nearly forty films, all B movies and almost all forgotten, with such titles as *Klondike Kate, The Crime Doctor's Man Hunt, The Return of Rusty*, and *New Orleans Uncensored*. Still, he always nurtured a talent for outrageous promotion. Even before entering the film business, he possessed an instinct for roping in customers that would have made P. T. Barnum proud. In the 1930s, while he was a struggling young theater director in a regional playhouse, Castle feared that his latest production was dying a quick death at the box office. Casting about for some way to grab the public's attention, he seized upon the fact that his lead actress had recently come to America from Nazi Germany. One night, after another poorly attended performance, Castle snuck back to the theater with an armful of bricks and a can of paint. He hurled the bricks through the windows and painted swastikas on the theater's walls. As Castle had hoped, this bogus act of Nazi vandalism captured newspaper headlines. From then on, the seats in the theater were filled.

He didn't find an outlet in the movie business for his ballyhoo talents until the late 1950s, when horror films became a big box-office draw, especially for young audiences looking for cheap thrills. And when it came to generating cheap thrills, William Castle was the man born for the job. His first horror film, *Macabre* (1958), was actually far from horrifying, but that didn't matter. With the savvy of an old-fashioned carnival barker, Castle knew that it was more important to create the *impression* that the film was going to be horrifying. And it wasn't enough to suggest merely that the movie was scary. The film had to be so scary that it was just about unbearable—or at least, Castle was going to challenge viewers to see for themselves. For this, he needed a gimmick.

What Castle came up with was a Lloyd's of London insurance policy, issued to every member of the audience, insuring the viewer against death by fright while watching the picture. Needless to say, nobody collected. (The movie was more likely to induce boredom than heart-stopping trauma.) As Castle hoped, though, the stunt grabbed people's attention and pulled in customers. More Castle horror films and more gimmicks would follow. For *House on Haunted Hill* he strung a luminescent plastic skeleton over the heads of the audience. For *Thirteen Ghosts* he provided a special viewing contraption equipped with two colored filters; through one filter the moviegoer could see the ghosts on screen, through the other the "chickenhearted" would be spared the supposedly terrifying sight. For *Mr. Sardonicus*, Castle appeared on screen and conducted a "Punishment Poll" during the final reel of the movie, in which he asked the audience to decide whether the film's villain should live or die (of course, since Castle's counting of the votes was already recorded on film, only one outcome was possible).

Matinee reproduces some of Castle's come-ons. The movie also stretches the truth a bit with a few stunts of its own. As the Lawrence Woolsey character readies his greatest premiere, we learn that one of his previous releases was augmented by a death-by-fright insurance policy, as had been the case with Castle's *Macabre*. Another earlier Woolsey film, on the other hand, was supposed to have hypnotized the audience. This was something Castle never attempted himself, although the gimmick was used by a Castle wannabe in *Horrors of the Black Museum* (1959). Along the same lines, Woolsey's newest picture is presented in Rumblerama, which literally shakes up the theater and audience. In actuality, this stunt was not attempted until 1974, with the release of the non-Castle disaster epic *Earthquake*, shown in floor-rumbling Sensurround.

The most striking Castle-ism in *Matinee* occurs during the premiere of Lawrence Woolsey's latest shock fest, *MANT* ("Half Man—Half Ant!"). The theater seats are wired with what seem to be electrical shock devices, which jolt the viewers during certain *MANT* high points. In 1959, Castle included this same gimmick in his presentation of the Vincent Price chiller *The Tingler*. Always fond of hifalutin terminology, he dubbed this cheap trick "Percepto." When the title creature, a rather unconvincing, oversized centipede, is set loose in a movie theater within the film, the seats buzzed to simulate a Tingler attack in the theater where the Vincent Price movie was being shown. The Percepto "process," however, differed from the *Matinee* gimmick in two ways. One, Castle zapped his viewers with vibrating motors rather than electric shockers. And two, Castle installed only a handful of motors per theater, while Woolsey wired every seat. No way Castle would have forked over the money to produce that good an effect.

Matinee takes even more artistic license when Woolsey's Atomovision kicks in. Unlike Castle's bald-faced come-ons, Atomovision appears to be a genuine process, a form of cinematic and stagecraft trickery that actually creates a convincing illusion and really does scare the hell out of the audience. In the final moments of *MANT*, an atom bomb seems to erupt outside the theater, sending a fireball through the screen, toward the audience, leaving a mushroom cloud exposed through what appears to be the demolished theater wall. Obviously, the low-budget Castle, whose strong suit was always chutzpah rather than technique, would never have even considered such an elaborate piece of showmanship. But he certainly would have approved of Atomovision's effect on the audience—complete and utter panic. William Castle always aimed for that response, even if his would-be shockers fell drastically short.

One more note: *MANT* is, in fact, a kind of movie that William Castle never attempted during the fifties and early sixties. Somehow he managed to get through this creature-crazy period without making a single mutant-bug picture. For some reason, he waited until 1975 to tackle this theme, when he produced his final film, *Bug*, a tale of brainy, firebreathing beetles on a rampage. The movie was released without a single promotional gimmick. But then, by this time, horror-movie watching was no longer the irresistibly hokey experience it was when Castle was in his heyday.

MOVIES ON MOVIE PEOPLE

For years, Hollywood has been fond of revealing itself on screen. In such films as *A Star Is Born* and *The Player,* the movie industry has aimed its cameras behind the scenes to tell stories about performers, directors, and studio executives, often in an unflattering or at least irreverent light. In many cases, the point of these backstage dramas seems to be that Hollywood is willing to present itself, warts and all. But often the filmmakers aren't quite up-front about exactly whom they're presenting. Schlockmeister William Castle, featured in disguised form in *Matinee,* is only one of many examples.

Here, in chronological order, are some other reel fictional makeovers of real movie people:

The Bad and the Beautiful (1952).

A glossy and engrossing tale of Hollywood ambition that includes a subplot about a troubled young actress named Georgia Lorrison. She leads a dissipated existence, living in the shadow of her celebrated father, a dashing leading man of both stage and screen. Portrayed by Lana Turner, she is modeled after Diana Barrymore, daughter of the great John Barrymore and heir to a prestigious theatrical clan's legacy. She committed suicide at the age of thirty-eight, eight years after this film was released. Diana's grandniece, incidentally, is current star Drew Barrymore, who has had some well-publicized troubles of her own.

The Goddess (1958).

Another starlet in trouble. In this Paddy Chayefsky–scripted film, a high-spirited small-town girl named Emily Ann Faulkner (played by Kim Stanley) goes to Hollywood and transforms herself into the sex symbol known as Rita Shawn. Anyone who has had their finger anywhere near the pulse of American pop culture should be able to guess that this character was inspired by a girl named Norma Jean Baker who became Marilyn Monroe.

(continued . . .)

Movies on Movie People

The Wild Party (1974).

An early Merchant/Ivory effort starring James Coco as an overweight silent-film comic named Jolly Grimm, who stages a lavish soiree to revive his sagging career. The night of Hollywood decadence ends in murder. A highly fictionalized take on silent star Fatty Arbuckle, accused of raping and causing the death of a young actress. A jury eventually acquitted him.

The Last Tycoon (1976).

Robert De Niro portrays an incisive, beleaguered young studio executive named Monroe Stahr, in this adaptation of F. Scott Fitzgerald's final, uncompleted novel. The character is modeled after Irving Thalberg, MGM's boy wonder from Hollywood's Golden Age, who died of pneumonia at age thirty-seven.

My Favorite Year (1982).

A farcical send-up of the great swashbuckler Errol Flynn. Going under the name Alan Swann, and played by Peter O'Toole, this quasi-Flynn is a falling-down-drunk and inveterate womanizer (accomplishments that certainly could have been found on the movie swordsman's résumé) who comes to New York in 1954 to guest-star on a TV comedy-variety show. The program is itself another true show-business allusion. Its star, played by Joseph Bologna, is a popular comedian named King Kaiser, clearly patterned after Sid Caesar.

White Hunter, Black Heart (1990).

Clint Eastwood stars as John Wilson, a boozy, womanizing director who goes on location in Africa to film a movie featuring a tough-guy star and a blue-blood leading lady. The film-within-the-film is an allusion to The African Queen, starring Humphrey Bogart and Katharine Hepburn. The director, who is more interested in shooting elephants than the picture, is a thinly veiled portrait of the iconoclastic John Huston.

Monsieur Verdoux

This **1948 comedy** is easily Charlie Chaplin's strangest film. Leaving his lovable Tramp far behind, he portrays a serial wife killer, a Parisian bigamist who juggles several spouses at once until he can devise ways of killing them for their money and possessions. Finding humor in such a cold-blooded character is offbeat in itself, especially for its time, but what makes the movie even more peculiar is that Chaplin, as writer-director as well as star, characterizes the murderous Verdoux as a wise, world-weary philosopher in a story that eventually turns into, of all things, an antiwar statement and a denunciation of capitalism.

When originally released, *Monsieur Verdoux* was clouded in controversy. Red-baiters were accusing Chaplin of Communist sympathies at the time, and jingoist picketers marched outside theaters showing the film. The growing anti-Red hysteria of the period was enough to cripple the movie's chance of attracting an audience. The odd subject matter didn't help. Amid all the right-wing protests, an intriguing fact about the film was often overlooked. The movie's philosophizing may have been purely Chaplin's creation, but Verdoux himself clearly sprang from an infamous murder case of the 1920s concerning a man named Henri Landru, also known as "The Bluebeard of Paris."

The parallels are striking. Like Verdoux, Landru was employed as a clerk before embarking on his career of murder for profit. Other facts Chaplin lifted from the Landru case included the killer's professional cover (he poses as a furniture dealer), his seemingly normal life apart from his homicidal activities (he keeps returning to an adoring wife and child), and his means of disposing of victims (he removes all traces of them of by reducing them to ashes in the incinerator at his country villa). But the process of turning his antihero into a tragic, reflective figure required that Chaplin steer away from the facts in some very crucial ways.

Verdoux, for most of his life, is a responsible, law-abiding citizen. He resorts to his murderous schemes only after he has been fired from his job in the midst of the Great Depression. In other words, his crimes are a solution—an *extreme* solution—to a personal and global economic crisis. Landru, on the other hand, was never a stranger to crime, even during his relatively respectable years as a clerk. Repeatedly he was arrested for fraud. During those interludes at large, between prison sentences, he was fond of seducing gullible women, impregnating them, and abandoning them. By the time he murdered his first lonely, rich woman, he was already an incorrigible swindler. He did not launch his murder spree during the Great Depression, and he was not taking desperate measures to overcome financial ruin. He began murdering women for their money during World War I. The Great War became his decoy. As long as the authorities were preoccupied with fighting the Kaiser, they weren't likely to notice Landru's much smaller-scale slaughter.

Toward the end of *Monsieur Verdoux*, Chaplin's murderer is sentenced to death and is asked if he has any statement to make on his behalf. The answer is yes, which should come as no surprise to anyone familiar with the former silent star's propensity for speechifying in his later films. He launches into a curious explanation for his crimes. "As for being a mass murderer," he tells the court, "does not the world encourage it?" Essentially, he argues that since there is such a thing as war, why bother condemning a man for killing people? Later on, Verdoux states that really he was just a businessman, no different from all other businessmen, who, it would seem, commit homicide on a regular basis. In the first half of the film, there are some brilliant black-comedy scenes of Chaplin bamboozling and doing away with his victims. But when he holds forth in the final reel, his supposedly ironic commentary on the human condition makes for specious philosophy and tedious viewing. In contrast, Henri Landru's true life of crime—an exercise in pure psychopathic ruthlessness with no redeeming sociological value whatever—is far more compelling.

Landru proved early on in his life that he could conjure up an upstanding appearance. He studied mechanical engineering at the age of sixteen and gave the impression that he was a serious young man intent upon a successful career in the white-collar world. After completing his studies, he enlisted in the army and achieved the rank of sergeant. Returning to civilian life, he then clerked in an architect's office, worked as a toy salesman, and even managed to become a subdeacon in his local church. He also took on the role of family man when he married in 1893 at the age of twenty-four. Of course, this particular badge of respectability was marred somewhat by the fact that his bride was his cousin and that he had sired a child with her out of wedlock before agreeing to matrimony.

The passion that truly drove him was his desire to separate people from their money. During his early career, at least, he doesn't seem to have been very good at it. Starting with his first arrest in 1891, his scams landed him in prison at regular intervals. By 1914, though, he had improved his technique. From then on he made sure that his swindle victims would never be able to testify against him.

He found his victims through ads he placed in newspapers. He announced in these ads that he was seeking marketable used furniture. When the person responding turned out to be an unattached woman of means, Landru turned on the charm. Bald and bearded, he looked more like an elf than a womanizer, but he must have possessed a powerful gift of gab. Courtship and marriage proposals followed. The woman's ultimate destination would be Landru's villa outside Paris. Once he was certain he could gain control of her possessions, he would murder the woman (the method has never been clearly established), then he would chop up the corpse and incinerate it in his stove. His disposal of the bodies was so thorough that the police never could produce a corpus delicti.

In five years, Landru murdered ten women, as well as one teenage boy, the son of one of the doomed brides who had the bad fortune of accompanying his mother to Landru's villa. As is the case in *Monsieur Verdoux*, the Bluebeard of Paris was captured after the relative of a victim spotted him in Paris and recognized him as the dead woman's husband. Without a corpse to prove that murder had even been committed, the prosecution relied on Landru's correspondence with his victims and a small account book of sorts, in which the Bluebeard kept track of his various lethal affairs. The court convicted him and sentenced him to death.

Another parallel between *Monsieur Verdoux* and Monsieur Landru: the real Bluebeard of Paris had some things to say on his behalf during his trial. He did not, however, have any thoughts on the viciousness of capitalism or the madness of global war. Like the classic sociopath that he was, he resorted to the most torturous logic to try eluding punishment. He couldn't fall back upon an insanity plea because doctors testified that he was legally sane. Instead, he seized upon this testimony as a possible loophole. If he was sane, Landru argued, then he could not have possibly committed these murders since they were obviously the work of a madman. Predictably, this argument impressed nobody. The closest Landru came to admitting anything occurred during a private conversation with the judge. He confessed to cheating on his wife 283 times. Otherwise, the Bluebeard of Paris maintained his innocence all the way to the guillotine.

A REAL NATURAL

Everything about *The Natural* makes it seem like a fairy tale, from the wondrously gifted baseball hero who literally smacks the cover off the ball, to the lightning-struck bat that seems to possess supernatural power, to the pure-of-heart heroine who ends the hero's hitting slump merely, and literally, by standing up for him. Indeed, the Bernard Malamud novel that inspired the film was fashioned as a twentieth-century myth, substituting a baseball star for the traditional warrior hero. But, like many myths and legends, this tale weaves real personalities and incidents into its fanciful narrative.

For Roy Hobbs, the story's larger-than-life hero, Malamud drew upon the game's most fantastic, outsized player. With his staggering strength and equally staggering appetites, Babe Ruth often seemed like a character out of a frontier tall tale himself, and was ideally suited as the model for a myth-like hero. In the film version, several of Malamud's Ruthian allusions were deleted, such as the scene of Hobbs pointing to the spot in the outfield bleachers where he is about to hit his next home run. But one similarity remains. As was true of the Sultan of Swat, Redford's Hobbs begins his career as a pitching phenom, then transforms himself into the sport's most prodigious slugger.

Hobbs's story, though, is not based solely on one baseball figure. Early in the film, for instance, his promising career is thrown off track when he visits the hotel room of an alluring mystery woman (Barbara Hershey) only to discover that she is a gun-wielding psycho. After she puts a bullet through his side, Hobbs plunges into obscurity for years before climbing back to the majors. This incident was clearly patterned after the shooting of Philadelphia Phillies first baseman Eddie Waitkus. Waitkus was on a tear at the time, hitting over .300 by late June of the 1949 season, when he responded to a note inviting him to the hotel room of a fan named Ruth Steinhagen. Once Steinhagen had Waitkus in the room, she produced a .22-caliber rifle and announced, "For two years you've been bothering me and now you're going

(continued . . .)

A Real Natural

to die." But the shot that pierced his right lung did not kill the first baseman. He recovered enough to return to the Phillies lineup the next season and played in the 1950 World Series.

In *The Natural,* when Roy Hobbs makes *his* return to Major League Baseball, he has to suffer the indignity of sitting on the bench for a last-place team. He finally gets his chance to play only when one of his teammates dies after crashing through the outfield wall. This is an allusion to Pete Reiser, a player of near Hobbsian ability himself, who led the Brooklyn Dodgers to a pennant in only his second season. Unfortunately, he also had the habit of running full tilt into outfield walls in pursuit of fly balls. He didn't die as a result, but the collisions effectively killed his career after only a few seasons.

There is one other piece of baseball lore that was a critical element in the book but was not carried over onto the movie screen. The film is an exercise in wish fulfillment—Redford is offered a bribe to throw a play-off game but in the end decides he can't betray the fans and goes on to clobber a momentous, game-winning home run. In Malamud's novel, however, Hobbs is ultimately a failed hero. He follows through on the bribe and throws the game. Here, Malamud was obviously invoking the painful memory of Shoeless Joe Jackson. One of the greatest hitters the sport has ever known, Jackson was disgraced by his involvement in the Black Sox Scandal of 1919, in which he and other White Sox players accepted bribes to take a dive in the World Series. In fact, the final, melancholy scene of the Malamud book is a virtual re-creation of Jackson's dramatic exit from a Chicago courtroom following his grand jury testimony—or, at least, a re-creation of the popular, perhaps apocryphal version of what happened on those courthouse steps. In both the Joe Jackson story and the Malamud novel, the fallen hero is confronted by a heartbroken boy. "Say it ain't so, Joe," the boy in Chicago supposedly said, while the child in Malamud's novel cries, "Say it ain't true, Roy."

On the Waterfront

O*n the Waterfront* is well grounded in fact. This should come as no surprise to anyone who has seen this 1954 Oscar winner. With its gritty photography, naturalistic performances, and authentic dockside locations, the film exudes a heightened sense of realism that makes it natural to believe that the story is an accurate depiction of waterfront life. And for good reason. The convincing illusion on screen was the result of several years of intensive research.

During this time, screenwriter Budd Schulberg befriended longshoremen along the New York and New Jersey piers, and day after day listened to their stories about brutal labor racketeers and their corrupt practices. As is shown in the film, the waterfront union forced workers to submit to tyrannical "shape-ups." Twice a day, longshoremen had to assemble on the docks before a union hiring boss who would choose a mere half or third of them to work. Those who did land a job had to deliver kickbacks to union officials. Those who didn't often had to accept money from union-sponsored loan sharks in order to support their families; they would then have to pay the money back at usurious rates. Goons pummeled anyone who questioned union authority and murdered anyone who threatened to testify against the racket. All this can be seen in the operations of Lee J. Cobb's Johnny Friendly in the Elia Kazan–directed film. But it was not only the general conditions on the waterfront that found their way into Schulberg's script. One man in particular also served as a model for a key character.

On screen, the courageous, tough-minded Father Barry, played by Karl Malden, provides the moral leadership for Terry Molloy (Marlon Brando) and other longshoremen anxious to make a stand against their union overseers. Schulberg based the character on a real waterfront priest who played a pivotal role in triggering harbor-union reforms. Named Father John Corridan, this man of the cloth was described by Schulberg as a "chain-smoking, ruddy-complexioned man in his early forties who looked fit enough to swing a hook with the best of them." While Malden's Father Barry amounted to art imitating life, Father Corridan, in turn, seemed to be a case of life imitating art. He was so principled, forthright, and streetwise that he seemed to have emerged from an old Warner Bros. movie, specifically one of those in which Pat O'Brien would play a priest who could alternately do God's work and swap snappy repartee with hardened street toughs.

Father Corridan came by his man-of-the-people image honestly. He grew up in the tenements of New York and knew firsthand what struggling city families had to contend with. His father, an Irish immigrant and a New York City cop, died when Corridan was nine. This left his mother with the job of supporting the family as a cleaning woman. The Jesuit order of the priesthood was Corridan's route out of the slums.

Father Corridan began his waterfront work in 1946, at the age of thirty-five, when he joined the St. Francis Xavier Labor School, near the west-side piers of Manhattan. Here, he instructed workers on the relevance of Christian principles in labor/management relations. As he learned about gangsterism and working conditions on the docks, his work became a crusade for honest trade unionism.

His first task was to gather information on the corrupt system governing waterfront life. In time, he assembled enough documents to fill sixteen file cabinets, while the facts and figures compiled in his head were enough to qualify him as a leading expert on the subject. During this period, the International Longshoremen's Association was dominated by such disreputable figures as Big Bill McCormick, Tough Tony Anastasio, and, further in the background, Tough Tony's brother, Albert Anastasia of Murder, Inc. Cooperating with the crooked union were the shipping companies, as well as many local government officials.

It wasn't always safe for dockworkers to show up at the Xavier School for Corridan's classes. Sometimes they had to sneak in through a back door to avoid being seen by union enforcers. Once, Father Corridan confronted a union henchman who had been assigned to disrupt his class. The priest gave the goon a talking-to that would have done either Pat O'Brien or Karl Malden proud, giving the hireling a message to take back to his bosses. The priest warned that "if anything happens to the men I'm trying to help here, I'll know who's responsible, and I'll personally see to it that they are broken throughout this port. They'll pay and I'll see that they pay."

Other memorable moments in Corridan's fight against gangsterism occurred during public pronouncements. One of them prefigured the emotionally powerful scene in *On the Waterfront* in which Father Barry delivers a sermon to workers in the hold of a ship. In his own sermon on the docks, Father Corridan expounded upon the presence of Christ on the waterfront: "I suppose some people would smirk at the thought of Christ in the shape-up. It is about as absurd as the fact that He carried carpenter's tools in His hands and earned His bread by the sweat of His brow. As absurd as the fact that Christ redeemed all men irrespective of their race, color, or station in life. It can be absurd only to those of whom Christ has said, 'Having eyes, they see not; and having ears, they hear not.' Because they don't want to see or hear. Christ also said, 'If you do it to the least of mine, you do it to me.' So Christ is in the shape-up."

Father Corridan's crusade began to produce results during the harbor wildcat strike of 1951. A rebel faction of dockworkers rejected a compromise contract agreement arranged by union leaders—an agreement imposed on the rank and file. To dramatize their grievances, the rebels closed down the New York/New Jersey ports for twenty-five days. Father Corridan conducted a public prayer at strike headquarters to strengthen the rebels' morale and to refute the cynical union charge that the strikers were Communists. Working with other reformers behind the scenes, he also pressured New York Governor Thomas Dewey to look into the issues raised by the strike. The priest knew that only state or federal officials could help; the local government was too compromised by organized-crime influence. Eventually Father Corridan's efforts led to a New York State investigation and the establishment of a joint New York/New Jersey commission to regulate the harbor business. Among its other reforms, the commission banned the hated shape-up.

Father Corridan stayed on the waterfront until 1957, three years after Karl Malden portrayed his fictional counterpart on screen. By that time he had been struggling for the dockworkers' cause for eleven years. His reward for his good works was a more reflective, leisurely job teaching economics at the Jesuits' LeMoyne College in Syracuse.

The Philadelphia Story

Some **"real-to-reel" movies** take situations based on actual events and place completely fictitious characters in them (Alfred Hitchcock's *Frenzy*, for example, uses a story drawn from fact—the true-crime case of "Jack the Stripper"—and populates it with wholly imaginary figures). Others do the opposite, taking characters based on real people and inventing totally made-up stories for them.

The latter is the case with the 1940 classic *The Philadelphia Story*, one of the most beloved films of Hollywood's "Golden Age." This sparkling romantic comedy began life as a hit Broadway play starring Katharine Hepburn, whose previous films had done so poorly with the public that she'd been branded "box-office poison" by *Variety*. In a canny career move, Hepburn bought the film rights to the play (written by Philip Barry), brought in director George Cukor, and handpicked her costars, Cary Grant and Jimmy Stewart. The resulting movie became a box-office smash, earned six Academy Award nominations, and instantly revived Hepburn's failing film career, turning her into a Hollywood icon.

Hepburn stars as Tracey Lord, the spoiled, high-spirited, sharp-tongued daughter of a super-rich Philadelphia family. The film begins with a famous wordless prologue, showing the breakup of her marriage to handsome C. K. Dexter Haven (Cary Grant). In a classic bit of physical comedy, the infuriated Grant—after cocking his fist as though to pop her in the snoot—sticks his hand on Hepburn's haughty face and shoves her to the floor.

The movie then cuts to the present. It is two years later, and Tracey is about to wed her second husband, the somewhat stuffy, self-made millionnaire George Kittredge (John Howard). Complications ensue when her first hubby, Dexter, unexpectedly shows up with a couple of people in tow—Macauley "Mike" Connor (Jimmy Stewart) and Liz Imbrie (Ruth Hussey). Posing as acquaintances of Tracey's absent brother, Mike and Liz are in reality a writer-photographer team for the gossip magazine *Spy*, who have been given the assignment of infiltrating Tracey's exclusive world and doing a tell-all tabloid piece.

The remainder of the movie—which takes place over the course of the single day (and night) leading up to the wedding, and is set entirely on the Lords' swanky estate—is a sophisticated screwball comedy in which Hepburn exerts an irresistible pull on all three of the male principals, who vie for her love. In the end, everything works out just the way it should, with the pompous Kittredge abandoned at the altar, Hepburn and Grant back in each other's arms, and Jimmy Stewart (who has been temporarily bedazzled by Tracey) reunited with the far more appropriate Liz.

Needless to say, none of the amusing shenanigans depicted in the film bears any resemblance to real life (if anything, the film has the magically romantic quality of a Shakespearean comedy like *As You Like It* or *A Midsummer Night's Dream*). There was, however, a true-life inspiration for the original play: Hope Montgomery Scott, a lovely, irrepressible Philadelphia heiress who served as the model for Hepburn's character, Tracey Lord.

In "Main Line Madcap," a 1995 article for *Vanity Fair* magazine, writer H. G. Bissinger provides a lively biography of the legendary socialite. Born in 1905, Hope Montgomery Scott "reigned for seventy years as the unofficial queen of Philadelphia's WASP oligarchy." Though she traveled around the world and partied with the most celebrated people of her day—lunching with Winston Churchill on Aristotle Onassis' yacht, singing for the Duke of Windsor at New York's Stork Club, dancing the Charleston in Paris with Josephine Baker—her primary residence throughout her life was Ardrossan, one of Main Line Philadelphia's most lavish estates.

Consisting of 750 picturesque acres, Ardrossan featured a fifty-room Georgian brick mansion with thirteen-foot ceilings, hallways as big as museum corridors, a dining-room table that could accommodate thirty-two people, and a permanent staff of twelve white-gloved servants. (The flawless behavior expected of the staff was epitomized, according to Bissinger, by the family butler, Oscar Hugo Larson, "who on a July night in 1952 served dinner in the impeccable fashion that had distinguished his 30-year tenure at Ardrossan. Then and only then, with his responsibilities fully discharged, did he turn his attention to his own affairs, which meant retiring to the pantry and shooting himself fatally in the head.")

In the midst of all this aristocratic polish and upper-class propriety, Hope Montgomery Scott stood out as a uniquely free-spirited individual who—for all her elegance and breeding—loved to talk dirty, stir up mischief, and party until dawn. "She seized each lively moment with almost maniacal intensity," Bissinger reports. Legendarily eccentric, she had a fondness for dirty jokes, bawdy Christmas cards, notepads with pornographic etchings, and shoes with liquid-filled Lucite heels.

At parties, she might sidle up to a male guest and confess that she liked to "look around the room to see who would be the most fun to sleep with." She was known to tool around her estate on a tractor while wearing a bikini top. When a friend fell ill and couldn't attend a dinner party, she sat her pet dog at the table in his place. Even in extreme old age, she maintained her irrepressible spirits. Interviewed at ninety, she chuckled over an injury she had sustained a year before, when—while opening a champagne bottle—the cork popped out and smacked her in the eye. Her death in July 1995 at age ninety marked the passing of an entire era, when the upper-crust families of Philadelphia's Main Line represented the very pinnacle of American snobbery and elitism.

Among the countless accomplished friends who hung out at Ardrossan during its heyday was the playwright Philip Barry, who not only got the inspiration for *The Philadelphia Story* from observing Hope but dedicated the play to her. Interestingly, when Barry's Broadway smash was turned into a movie, Hollywood—in a reversal of its normal procedure—made the reality seem *less* glamorous. The actual lifestyle enjoyed by the true-life Tracey Lord was simply too extravagant to seem credible. As Bissinger writes, "the moviemakers were convinced that Americans could never accept the idea that there were those among their fellow countrymen who lived on a scale so grand, lavish, and European."

A Place in the Sun

At the time of its release in 1951, George Stevens's engrossing adaptation of Theodore Dreiser's classic crime novel, *An American Tragedy* (which had been filmed once before, in 1931) earned widespread critical acclaim, including the Directors Guild of America Award, a Golden Globe for Best Drama of the Year, and six Oscars. Los Angeles film critic Charles Champlin called it unequivocally "the best film ever to come out of Hollywood." Though Champlin's praise seems inflated today (on the American Film Institute's controversial list of the one hundred best Hollywood movies of all time, *A Place in the Sun* ranks number ninety-two), the film still retains its power, thanks largely to the first-rate performances of its three stars, Montgomery Clift, Shelley Winters, and Elizabeth Taylor.

The story concerns an ambitious, if socially insecure, young man named George Eastman (Clift), who has been offered a job by a rich uncle, the owner of a booming bathing-suit company. In the very first scene, we see George hitchhiking along the highway, on his way to his new life. Suddenly he notices a roadside advertisement for his uncle's swimwear: a billboard of a dark-haired bathing beauty, posing provocatively on the beach. The picture represents everything that George

149

(who comes from a poor, fundamentalist background) most desperately yearns for: all the pleasure and luxury and freedom of the American Dream.

It isn't long before he meets the living embodiment of that dream in the form of a wealthy young beauty named Angela Vickers (Elizabeth Taylor at her most youthfully radiant). Eventually, the handsome young man and the ravishing debutante fall madly in love. Everything that George hungers for seems within his grasp: money, social position, and the love of the world's most beautiful woman.

Unfortunately, there is just one small problem. By that point, George—who has been working his way up from the assembly line—has already impregnated Alice Tripp, a factory girl he got involved with when he first came to work. As portrayed to perfection by Shelley Winters, "Al" is the absolute antithesis of Angela. Though endowed with a crude sensuality, she is dumpy, whiny, and even poorer than George. Instead of a life filled with comfort, glamour, and erotic passion, she offers a future involving a large brood of runny-nosed children, crushing poverty, and the constant complainings of a fat, nagging wife. Not surprisingly, when she demands that George marry her, his thoughts turn to murder.

Suggesting an outing to a remote wilderness lake, he takes her for a ride in a rowboat with the intention of drowning her. But at the last minute, he changes his mind and decides to do the right thing by Alice. Ironically, when she gets up to embrace him, the boat overturns, and Alice—who can't swim—drowns. George makes it to shore and, in a panic, tries to flee. He is arrested, tried for murder (by a pre–*Perry Mason* Raymond Burr as the most fanatical prosecutor since *Les Misérables'* Javert), convicted, and sent to the electric chair—though not before a soul-searching scene in which he acknowledges his guilt for not having done more to save the drowning girl.

Though the movie somewhat oversimplifies the issues of Dreiser's book (essentially reducing George's predicament to a choice between rich, gorgeous, adoring Elizabeth Taylor and penniless, dowdy, annoying Shelley Winters), it does suggest the larger social themes that Dreiser was interested in when he wrote *An American Tragedy*. As

Dreiser explained in a 1935 magazine article, while working as a reporter in 1892, he "began to observe a certain type of crime in the United States. It seemed to spring from the fact that almost every young person was possessed of an ingrowing ambition to be somebody financially and socially." The kind of crime he was referring to involved the "young ambitious lover of some poorer girl who in the earlier state of affairs had been attractive enough to satisfy him, both in the manner of her love and her social station. But nearly always with the passing of time and the growth of experience on the part of the youth, a more attractive girl with money or social position appeared." In order to get rid of the first girl—who refused to let him go, often because she was pregnant—the young man resorted to murder. To Dreiser, this kind of crime was a distinctly American phenomenon, symptomatic of our country's diseased obsession with "making it" at all costs.

Dreiser began keeping his eyes peeled for a real-life crime that matched this model. He considered the cases of several cold-blooded fortune hunters: a medical intern named Harris who poisoned his penniless first wife so he could marry an attractive society woman; a Baptist minister named Richsen who impregnated a young parishioner, then killed her in order to marry a wealthy woman; and an amateur chemist named Molineux who—competing for the hand of a lovely young socialite—sent a box of poisoned candy to another of her suitors. The case Dreiser finally settled on—and that became the basis for his bestselling book and the subsequent movies—was one of the most sensational of its day, the Chester Gillette/Grace Brown murder case of 1906.

Gillette, a strikingly handsome young man, was the son of religious zealots. His upbringing had been marked by both poverty and instability, as his parents—missionaries for the Salvation Army—frequently moved from post to post, continually uprooting him. Thanks to the generosity of a wealthy relative, he was able to spend several years in prep school, where he gained a veneer of social polish.

After working for a while as a railroad brakeman, Gillette took a job at his uncle's skirt factory in Cortland, New York. There he became acquainted with—and eventually seduced—a pretty, nineteen-year-old factory girl named Grace Brown, the daughter of a local farmer. In the spring of 1906, Grace discovered that she was pregnant. By then, however, Chester's life had changed. He had begun to socialize with a much classier crowd, including a lovely young woman named Harriet Benedict, the daughter of a prominent lawyer.

When Grace insisted that Chester stick by her, he arranged for a trip to the Adirondacks. Immediately after their arrival at Big Moose Lake in Herkimer County, he rented a skiff and took her rowing. When they didn't return by the following morning, the boat's owner went in search of them and found the skiff floating upside down in a deserted section of the lake called Punkey Bay. Grace's corpse was discovered at the bottom of the lake. Chester—who had escaped through the woods— was quickly arrested. His trial in November 1906 was a nationwide sensation (so many reporters covered the proceedings that a special telegraph office had to be set up in the courthouse to handle their dispatches). Vigorously (not to say rabidly) prosecuted by a politically motivated DA, Gillette was convicted of first-degree murder and sentenced to death. Though his mother mounted a desperate campaign to save his life, he was executed at Auburn Prison in 1907.

Clearly, there are very close parallels between this true-life case and *A Place in The Sun*, though there are also major differences. The real Chester Gillette—an incorrigible cad who seems to have cared about nothing but his own pleasure—was a far less sympathetic figure than the sensitive (not to say tormented) character portrayed by Montgomery Clift. Moreover, while the movie makes it clear that "George" undergoes a last-minute change of heart and that "Alice" herself causes the fatal accident, the ultimate truth about Grace Brown's death remains somewhat ambiguous. Chester himself claimed that Grace had committed suicide. (At his trial, he testified that she had "jumped into the lake—stepped up onto the boat and kind of throwed herself in.") It is also conceivable that the boat capsized by accident. The evidence that Gillette had both plotted and caused her death, however, was so compelling that it took the jury just a few hours to convict him.

Most important, perhaps, there is no real counterpart to the Elizabeth Taylor character in the actual story. While Chester Gillette and

Harriet Benedict did have a few dates, their relationship appears to have been entirely casual. In the Hollywood version, it's almost possible to sympathize with—if not condone—George's feelings (particularly if you're a man). Faced with the choice between the gloriously beautiful, inconceivably wealthy Elizabeth Taylor and the hopelessly drab, impossibly whiny Shelley Winters, who wouldn't prefer the former? But in real life, Chester Gillette got rid of his pregnant girlfriend simply because she was an inconvenience—because she threatened to interfere with his fun.

Psycho

Truffaut: I've read the novel from which *Psycho* was taken . . . I believe it was based on a newspaper story.

Hitchcock: It was the story of a man who kept his mother's body in his house, somewhere in Wisconsin.

—Alfred Hitchcock interviewed by François Truffaut

A **beautiful blonde** slides out of her bathrobe, steps into the shower, and turns on the water. She pulls the plastic curtain closed. The water gushes down. She soaps herself, smiling. Suddenly, over her shoulder, a shadow appears on the other side of the curtain. It draws nearer. The curtain rips back. The shadow, shaped like an old woman, clutches a butcher knife. The big blade slashes downward, then slashes again. And again. The screeching chords on the sound-track match the dying shrieks of the victim as her streaming blood whirlpools down into the drain.

The sequence, of course, is the famous shower scene from Alfred Hitchcock's *Psycho*—the most frightening moment from the most influential horror movie of modern times. After *Psycho*, a new kind of monster began stalking the movie screens of America—the psychotic "slasher." And showering was never the same again.

The brilliance of Hitchcock's film derives from his genius for drawing us into a world of total insanity—a nightmare realm where a bathroom becomes a chamber of horrors, a shy young man changes into a crazed transvestite, and a sweet, little old lady turns out to be a mummified corpse. By the time the film is over, the shaken audience steps away from the screen saying "Thank God it was only a movie."

Perhaps the scariest thing about *Psycho*, then, is this—

It was based on the truth. There really was a maniac whose unspeakable deeds served as the inspiration for *Psycho*. His name wasn't Norman Bates, however. It was Edward Gein.

Gein grew up on a hardscrabble farmstead a few miles outside of Plainfield, Wisconsin, a small, featureless town situated in an area that has been called the "Great Dead Heart" of the state. His father, George, was a hard-luck type with a weakness for alcohol. Though George could be brutal when drunk, he was no match for his domineering wife, Augusta.

But then, it's hard to imagine how *anyone* could have matched Augusta's ferocious willpower. Or her all-consuming madness.

Raised in a fiercely religious atmosphere, she had gradually developed into a ranting fanatic who harped on a single theme—the loathsomeness of sex. Looking around at the world, all she perceived was rottenness and filth. She had fled the city of La Crosse—the place of Eddie's birth—because she regarded it as a modern day Sodom, reeking of sin and perversion. But Plainfield, in her warped view, had turned out to be no better. The small, God-fearing town was, in her eyes, a hellhole of depravity. She kept her two boys—Ed and his older brother, Henry—tightly bound to her apron strings and imbued them with her own twisted sense of universal wickedness, the whorish ways of women, and the vileness of carnal love.

When George Gein dropped dead of a heart attack in 1940, no one—not even his family—was sorry to see him go. Left alone with their mother, the two boys fell even more powerfully under her poisonous spell. Henry, at least, seems to have had some sense of Augusta's destructive influence and tried to help his brother break away. But Eddie wouldn't listen. He worshiped Augusta and did not take kindly to his brother's criticisms.

In 1944, Henry was found dead on the Geins' property—presumably from a heart attack while putting out a brushfire, though no one ever came up with a convincing explanation for the strange bruises on the back of his skull.

Now Eddie had his mother all to himself. But not for very long. In 1945, Augusta suffered a stroke. Eddie tended her night and day, though nothing he did ever seemed to be good enough. Sometimes— her voice slurred but still dripping with contempt—she would call him a weakling and a failure, just like his father. At other times, she would beckon him to her side and pat the mattress beside her. Eddie would crawl into bed and cling to her while she cooed into his ear—he was her own little man, her baby. At night, he wept himself to sleep, praying to God to spare his mother's life. Eddie knew he could never manage life without her—she had told him so herself.

But his prayers went unheeded.

A few months later, Augusta was stricken with another, even more devastating stroke. She died in December 1945. Eddie Gein, thirty-nine years old, was left all alone in his dark, empty, shut-off world.

It was then that he began his descent into the chaos of unutterable madness. But for a long time, no one seemed to notice. How could Ed's sickness have gone unrecognized so long in a town as small as Plain-field? There are several answers. A loner all his life, Ed started keeping even more to himself—locked up behind the weather-beaten walls of his gloomy, ramshackle farmhouse. And even when he did venture out in public—to run an errand in town or perform some handyman chores or drink an occasional beer at Mary Hogan's roadside tavern—he didn't seem any stranger than before. A little dirtier maybe and more in need of a bath, but he had always been a queer one, ever since childhood. Folks just accepted Eddie's peculiarities.

True, he seemed to talk more and more about the magazine articles he was so fascinated by—stories of Nazi atrocities and South Sea head-hunters and sex-change operations. And then there were the "jokes" he told. When Mary Hogan, the big, foulmouthed tavern keeper, suddenly disappeared from her place one afternoon, leaving nothing behind but a puddle of blood, Eddie began kidding that she was staying over at his house. But that kind of sick humor was just something you'd expect from a weirdo like Eddie Gein.

Even the stories about the creepy things at his farmhouse didn't faze most folks. Some neighborhood kids, who had visited his home, claimed that they had seen shrunken heads hanging from the walls of Eddie's bedroom. Eventually the rumors got back to Eddie, who had a plausible explanation. The heads, he said, were World War II souvenirs, sent to him by a cousin who had served in the South Seas. The neighbors just shrugged. Trust Eddie Gein to have weird souvenirs like that.

They never imagined that Eddie himself was capable of hurting anyone. Hell, the meek little man with the lopsided grin couldn't stand the sight of blood. He wouldn't even go deer hunting, like every other man in town.

That's what folks said. And then Bernice Worden disappeared.

It happened on November 16, 1957—the first day of deer-hunting season. Late that afternoon, Frank Worden returned from a fruitless day in the woods and proceeded directly to the corner hardware store owned and managed by his mother, Bernice, a fifty-eight-year-old widow. To his surprise, his mother wasn't there. Searching the premises, Worden discovered a trail of dried blood leading from the storefront out the back door. He also discovered a sales receipt for a half gallon of antifreeze made out to Mrs. Worden's last customer—Eddie Gein.

When the police arrived at Eddie's farmhouse to question him about Mrs. Worden's whereabouts, they came upon the body of the fifty-eight-year-old grandmother in the summer kitchen behind the house. Hanging by her heels from a pulley, she had been beheaded and disemboweled—strung up and dressed out like a butchered deer.

The stunned and sickened officers called for reinforcements. Before long, a dozen or more lawmen showed up at the farm and began exploring the unspeakable contents of Ed Gein's house of horrors. What they found during that long, hellish night was appalling beyond belief.

Soup bowls made from the sawed-off tops of human skulls. Chairs upholstered in human flesh. Lamp shades fashioned of skin. A boxful of noses. A belt made of female nipples. A shade pull decorated with a pair of woman's lips. A shoe box containing a collection of preserved female genitalia. The faces of nine women, carefully dried, stuffed with paper, and mounted, like hunting trophies, on a wall. A skin vest, complete with breasts, which had been fashioned from the tanned upper torso of a middle-aged woman.

Later, Eddie confessed that, at night, he would lace the skin around himself and go mincing around the farmhouse, pretending he was his mother.

At around 4:30 A.M., after much searching through the ghastly clutter of Gein's home, an investigator discovered a bloody burlap sack shoved under a fetid mattress. Inside was a freshly severed head. Two ten-penny nails, each with a loop of twine tied to the end of it, had been inserted into the ears. The head was Bernice Worden's. Eddie Gein was going to hang it up on the wall as a decoration.

At first, everyone assumed Eddie Gein had been running a murder factory. But during his confessions, he made a claim that seemed, at first, too incredible to accept. He wasn't a mass murderer at all, he insisted. Yes, he had killed two women—Bernice Worden and the tavern keeper Mary Hogan, whose preserved, peeled-off face had been found among Ed's gruesome collection. But as for the rest of the body parts, Eddie revealed that he had gotten them from local cemeteries. For the past twelve years, ever since his mother's death, he had been a grave robber, turning to the dead for the companionship he could not find among the living.

In the strict definition of the term, Eddie Gein was not a serial killer. He was a ghoul.

Gein spent the remainder of his days locked away in mental institutions. Long before his death from cancer at the age of seventy-eight, he had been immortalized in Alfred Hitchcock's *Psycho*, based on a novel whose author—Robert Bloch—had been inspired by the Gein affair. When Eddie died on July 26, 1984, they took his body back to Plainfield and buried it next to his mother. Eddie Gein was back where he belonged.

ED GEIN, SUPERSTAR

Among film buffs, Gein is legendary not only as the "real Norman Bates" but as the direct inspiration for several other celebrated horror films, primarily *The Texas Chainsaw Massacre,* and *The Silence of the Lambs.*

Tobe Hopper, the director of *The Texas Chainsaw Massacre,* reportedly heard stories about Gein from midwestern relatives and grew up haunted by these tales. In his splatter-movie classic, the Gein-inspired character is not a mild-mannered motel keeper with a split personality but a bestial hulk named Leatherface, who sports a mask made of dried human flesh.

Thomas Harris, author of *The Silence of the Lambs,* researched the FBI's files on Gein before creating his fictional serial killer, Jame Gumb (aka "Buffalo Bill"), a transsexual wanna-be who attempts to fashion a suit from the flayed torsos of his victims.

Psycho, Chainsaw, and *Silence* all take considerable liberties with the Gein story. The film that sticks closest to the facts is a 1974 low-budget shocker called *Deranged,* which has developed a major cult following among horror buffs.

Besides these movies, there are any number of Grade-Z gore films about mild-mannered hicks who turn out to be cannibalistic butchers—films with titles like *Invasion of the Blood Farmers* and *I Dismember Mama.* Indeed, it can be argued that the Gein story gave rise to the entire modern genre of "slasher" movies. Truly, if there can be such a thing as a "seminal psycho," Ed Gein fits the bill.

Raiders of the
Lost Ark

First and foremost, *Raiders of the Lost Ark* was inspired by adventure serials from the thirties and forties. As kids, both producer George Lucas and director Steven Spielberg were enthralled by the frantic exploits staged in such chapter plays as *Spy Smasher, Tailspin Tommy,* and *Don Winslow of the Navy. Raiders* was their attempt, obviously a successful one, to recapture that sort of boyish, wide-eyed excitement. Like heroes of the old cliffhangers, Indiana Jones races headlong from one supercharged predicament to another, relying on his wits, his fists, and his extraordinary fortitude to escape danger and accomplish colossal deeds single-handedly.

Secondarily, Lucas and Spielberg also drew upon accounts of Nazi obsessions with ancient religious artifacts, which the Third Reich believed would endow Germany's new empire with supernatural powers. From this came Indie's running battle with Nazi agents to retrieve the long-lost Ark of the Covenant.

As for the character of Indiana Jones himself, the daring archaeologist-adventurer, some believe an inspiration came from a little-remembered historical figure from the early 1800s. Archaeologists aren't known for projecting swashbuckling personas, but one man who did was a flamboyant Italian named Giovanni Belzoni. He may not have dodged runaway boulders or skirmished with blowgun-wielding tribesmen, but he was truly a larger-than-life character in every sense of the term. A towering man who stood six feet seven inches tall, he was at various times a circus performer, an author, and an inventor. He is best known, though, for risking life and limb to unearth some of the greatest treasures of ancient Egypt.

Born in 1778, Giovanni Battista Belzoni came from a prosaic background that offered no hint of the restless, audacious life that he would lead. He grew up in the ancient northern Italian town of Padua, where his father worked quietly as a barber. When he was a teenager, Belzoni fluctuated in his education between religion and science, studying for the priesthood for a while as well as taking instruction in the burgeoning technology of hydraulics. But as unexceptional as his early years were, he lived in tumultuous times that would prod him in new directions.

The French Revolution began when Belzoni was eleven years old. The upheavals were not confined to France but spread throughout Western Europe as the new regime battled neighboring nations. It was a time that could change the course of someone's life quickly and dramatically. Belzoni began his own unique journey through this era in 1796, when he was eighteen. In that year, the French government dispatched Napoleon and his troops to drive the Austrians out of northern Italy. Choosing to sidestep this conflict, Belzoni left his native country and began to drift, first across the continent, then into England. His training as a hydraulics engineer eventually led him into show business. He designed a system of pumps for what were then called water plays, elaborate displays of colored cascading water. Capitalizing on his enormous physique, he then joined an English circus act and performed staggering feats of strength. He would wear a special metal harness upon which other performers would climb. He could support the weight of twelve people stacked on top of him in a human pyramid, only the first kind of pyramid that would be associated with him. The

ancient architectural variety would come into his life when he rein-
vented himself during a trip to the Middle East.

Belzoni was traveling across the Mediterranean at the time, barnstorming from Sicily to Constantinople with his own theatrical troupe.
On the island of Malta, he discovered a new venture that interested him
more than novelty acts. He met an agent of Egypt's Pasha Mohammed
Ali. The pasha was intent upon bringing new technology to his country,
and Belzoni, always a quick hydraulics tinkerer, came up with a new
irrigation system involving an ingeniously designed waterwheel. The
idea was good enough to earn him a trip to Egypt. In the end, his invention would be rejected because it would put too many people out of
work, but the ever-adaptable Belzoni latched onto yet another venture.
This one would clinch his fame.

In Cairo, he met a kindred adventurous spirit, an explorer swathed
in Arabic robes named Sheikh Ibrahim bin Abd Allah. Actually, the man
was Swiss and his real name was Johann Ludwig Burckhardt. But what
was most important to Belzoni were the stories the "sheikh" told of
mysterious treasures along the Nile River, the most intriguing being a
gigantic head hacked out of stone that lay half-buried in the desert
sands. Belzoni wangled a commission to collect these artifacts on
behalf of the British consul.

The giant head, the first of Belzoni's great finds, was a likeness of
Ramses II. Belzoni found it outside the city of Thebes, and through a
system of levers and rollers he managed to convey the enormous bust
across the desert to the Nile and from there floated it on a raft downriver to Cairo. At the age of thirty-seven, he had finally found his great
calling in life.

Belzoni was the first modern European to explore the fabled Valley
of the Kings, where he excavated the tomb of Seti I, already three thousand years old. He discovered the secret passageway that led into the
central chamber of the Second Pyramid at Giza. He journeyed eastward
to the Red Sea and found the ruins of the lost city of Berenice. Through
it all, he braved the harshest conditions in a part of the world where
temperatures could soar to 120 degrees in the shade. He contended
with obstacles in human form as well.

Belzoni was not the only treasure-hunting Egyptologist at the time. The competition for priceless artifacts could be fierce. Belzoni's chief rival was the French consul general (an echo of the character Belloq, Indiana Jones's scheming French nemesis in *Raiders*). To seize the greatest treasures, Belzoni had to outwit and outrun the French and their henchmen. Once, while transporting a highly valuable obelisk, he found himself in a true Indie-style predicament. He and his men had ferried the obelisk downriver as far as Luxor when they were suddenly surrounded and held at gunpoint by a band of Arabs hired by the French. The henchmen made it clear they were going to murder Belzoni and his party in order to get the obelisk. Indiana Jones, of course, would have found some way to vanquish his adversaries, no matter how outnumbered he was. But Belzoni didn't enjoy the advantage of an action-movie mastermind like Spielberg to orchestrate his exploits. Instead, he was content to scuffle with the Arabs and make a hairbreadth getaway.

After returning to England and publishing a bestselling account of his Egyptian escapades, Belzoni was consumed by wanderlust once again. He ended up dying as he had lived, as an intrepid, globe-trotting adventurer. In December 1823, he died from dysentery and tropical fever while exploring the Niger River in search of the legendary city of Timbuktu.

Rampage

This **1992 psycho** thriller is one of those rare Hollywood productions that could have profited from an extra dose of raw sensationalism. It's definitely worth a look—but if you're a hard-core horror fan, you are likely to find it a frustrating experience. Writer-director William Friedkin—*auteur* of *The Exorcist*—certainly knows how to deliver the shocks, and *Rampage* contains just enough of them to suggest that this film could have been every bit as creepy as, say, David Fincher's *Seven*. Every time the proceedings threaten to become really scary, however, the film switches gears and becomes a talky manifesto on behalf of capital punishment. In the end, the movie suffers from a split personality. Half hair-raising splatter movie, half plodding courtroom drama, it ultimately seems as mixed up as its schizoid central character. Watching it is a little like sitting in front of the tube and switching back and forth between *The Silence of the Lambs* and Court TV.

It begins promisingly enough: a handsome young man with long brown hair and sunglasses strolls up to a tidy suburban home and knocks on the front door. When a sweet little old lady answers, he cheerfully shoots her in the head, then guns down her husband and adult daughter. Dragging the latter's still-living body to the upstairs bedroom, he proceeds to butcher it in unspeakable ways. When the police come upon the crime scene, the entire room is literally awash in gore.

The perpetrator turns out to be an amiable young psycho named Charles Reece (Alex McArthur), who suffers from the delusion that his body has been poisoned and that he must replenish his strength by slaughtering innocent people in his Stockton, California, neighborhood and drinking their blood (there is also the suggestion that he performs hideous sex acts on them). In the course of the movie, he commits these atrocities upon a middle-aged mother, her eight-year-old son, and (in a harrowing scene with strong echoes of *The Exorcist*) a Catholic priest. Ultimately, he is tracked down, captured, and put on trial.

While all of this is very unsettling (the sequence in which the cops break into Reece's cellar—a nightmarish lair full of preserved human organs, Nazi regalia, sadomasochistic porn, etc.—is especially strong), the movie's main (and far less compelling) focus is on a liberal-minded district attorney, Anthony Fraser (Michael Biehn), who starts off as a staunch opponent of the death penalty but who undergoes a dramatic change of heart as he delves ever deeper into Reece's twisted behavior.

Rampage begins with a title card announcing that the film was "inspired by true events." And, indeed, Friedkin's villain is a thinly disguised version of Richard Chase, one of the sickest multiple murderers of modern times. As appalling as the crimes of the fictitious Charles Reece are, they pale by comparison to the true-life atrocities of the young madman who became known as "The Vampire of Sacramento."

Born in 1950, Chase was raised in a highly unstable household. Even as a child, he displayed symptoms of severe emotional disturbance, including a precocious pyromania (a classic psychological warning sign). In high school, he became a serious abuser of alcohol and drugs, a situation that only exacerbated his rapidly deteroriating mental state.

By the time he reached his early twenties, Chase was in the grip of a profound and progressively dangerous form of psychosis. He heard voices in his head, carried on loud conversations with invisible beings, and became convinced that he was suffering from a host of bizarre afflictions. In 1973, he showed up at a Sacramento hospital, complaining of "cardiac arrest." When questioned by the emergency-room physicians, he insisted that his blood flow had stopped because someone had stolen his pulmonary artery.

By 1976, his delusions had become even more extreme. He began to believe that he was the reincarnation of a notorious western outlaw. He took to sleeping with oranges beside his head, so that "the vitamin C would filter into his brain." He was also subject to increasingly violent and uncontrollable outbursts.

Somewhere around this time, Chase—convinced that he needed fresh blood to keep his body from "falling apart"—became a vampire. At first, he obtained his supply from pet-shop rabbits. Bringing them home, he would disembowel them alive, eat their meat and viscera raw, and drink their blood. In April 1976, he was taken to the hospital after becoming violently ill from a self-administered injection of rabbit blood.

Eventually, Chase was transferred to a mental hospital, where (like the zoophilic Renfield in Bram Stoker's *Dracula*), he continued to batten on whatever small creatures—primarily birds—he could get his hands on. After less than six months of treatment, however, he was discharged into his parents' care. Though staff psychiatrists diagnosed him as a paranoid schizophrenic, they concluded (with, as it turned out, stunning inaccuracy) that he was not dangerous to others.

Before long, Chase—increasingly convinced that his body was rotting inside—reverted to his vampiric ways. Obtaining cats and puppies by any means possible—buying them from pet stores, stealing them from neighbors, adopting them from animal shelters—he would butcher them alive, mix their blood and organs in a blender (sometimes adding a splash of Coca-Cola for added flavor), and imbibe the nauseating concoction as though it were a health-food smoothie. Working his way up to ever-larger animals, he was picked up by police in August 1977 after eviscerating a cow.

Four months later, in early December 1977, Chase purchased a .22-caliber semiautomatic pistol. (As in Friedkin's movie, all the young maniac had to do to obtain this weapon was answer no to a few perfunctory queries, like "Are you a mental patient?" and "Have you ever been found by a court of law to be a danger to others as a result of a mental disorder?") By the end of the month, Chase was cruising around the streets, taking potshots at total strangers and killing his first human victim, a man named Ambrose Griffin, who was gunned down at random while strolling home from the supermarket.

Less than one month after the Griffin murder, Chase—after a chaotic morning of attempted break-ins at several neighborhood homes—entered the house of a twenty-two-year-old woman named Theresa Wallin, who was three months pregnant at the time. After shooting her three times, he dragged the dying woman into the master bedroom. What happened next has been graphically described by courtroom psychiatrist Ronald Markman in his 1989 book, *Alone with the Devil:*

> *He pushed her sweater and bra up out of the way, exposing her breasts, and then pulled down her pants, exposing her pubic region. Then he got a carving knife from the kitchen and went to work.*
>
> *While she was still alive, but most likely unconscious, Richard cut her open from chest to umbilicus, then pulled out her spleen and loop after loop of her intestines, which he dropped to the floor. He stabbed her liver, cut her diaphragm, severed one lung, sliced her pancreas in two, cut out both kidneys and put them on the bed, and then stabbed her in the heart. Then he stabbed her through her left nipple and thrust the knife repeatedly through the same opening. He smeared her blood all over his face and hands and licked it off his rubber-gloved fingers. As he tasted her blood, he pulled her left leg out of her pants, spread her legs, and made blood smears all over her inner thighs. He dipped a yogurt container into her blood and drank it, then crumpled the cup and left it next to her body. Finally, he defecated and stuffed feces into her mouth.*

After washing up in the bathroom, Chase left.

Four days later, he struck again. Barging into the home of twenty-seven-year-old Evelyn Miroth, he whipped out his pistol and shot her in the head. Hearing the sound, her fifty-year-old boyfriend, Daniel Meredith, and her six-year-old son, Jason, rushed from the living room and were immediately gunned down, then executed with bullets to their skulls.

Dragging the mortally wounded woman into the bedroom, Chase discovered a two-year-old baby—Miroth's nephew, David Ferreira—asleep in a playpen. Little David, too, was dispatched with a bullet to the head. Chase then proceeded to savage the dying woman's body in much the same way that he had mutilated Theresa Wallin's. After draining her blood into a pail and drinking some from a coffee cup, he carried the dead baby into the bathroom and opened the infant's skull with a kitchen knife, spilling some of the brains into the sink.

Just then, a caller arrived at the front door. Chase slipped out of the house, taking the infant's body with him. Smuggling it into his apartment, he picked up his ghastly handiwork where he had left off, slicing open the child's abdomen and removing the organs, drinking the blood, eating the brains.

The next day—following a tip from a suspicious neighbor—police entered Chase's apartment and discovered a chamber of horrors, rank with decay. The floors were caked with dried blood and excrement. Snapshots of human viscera hung on the walls. On the bed lay a dinner plate with a serving of brain tissue swimming in a sauce of fresh blood. The refrigerator held a half-gallon container filled with internal organs. Chase was immediately placed under arrest.

At first, he stoutly denied that he'd ever committed murder, insisting that the remains in his apartment came exclusively from butchered dogs. Nor would he reveal the whereabouts of the missing two-year-old baby. (Little David's decomposed corpse—concealed inside a cardboard box—would be found in a vacant lot several months later.) Eventually, however, Chase revealed that he'd committed the killings because he believed he was suffering from blood poisoning and needed human blood to stay alive.

Community feeling ran so high against the Vampire of Sacramento (as the tabloids dubbed him) that his defense was granted a change of venue. His trial began in January 1979 in San Jose. The young man's behavior was so extravagantly bizarre that even one of the psychia-

trists brought in by the prosecution concluded that he was insane. Nev-
erthless, on May 8, 1979, Chase was convicted of first-degree murder,
adjuged to be sane, and sentenced to death.

While *Rampage* concludes with the killer declared legally insane and
immured behind bars for an indeterminate stretch of time, the movie's
real-life model came to a very different end. On Christmas Eve 1979—
after secretly saving up his daily medication for a period of time—Chase
killed himself with a massive overdose of his prescribed antipsychotic.

The Roaring Twenties

James Cagney, bullet-ridden and mortally wounded, staggers down a snow-blanketed city block, stumbles headlong to a church entrance, and finally tumbles and sprawls across the stone steps. Gladys George, as a frowsy saloon singer, reaches his side and gathers him in her arms. When a cop asks her who the dead man is, she replies forlornly that his name is Eddie Bartlett. "He used to be a big shot," she says. One of the most famous death scenes in film history, this sequence brings to an end *The Roaring Twenties*, part of the memorable pack of films that made 1939 such a spectacular year in Hollywood.

Although regarded today as one of Cagney's definitive gangster pictures, the original author saw it not as a crime melodrama so much as a social history of an extraordinary era. Mark Hellinger was one of the most renowned newspapermen of his day, a New York columnist who, along with Damon Runyon and Walter Winchell, defined America's conception of the brassy, colorful Broadway scene. When he was hired by

Warner Bros. in the late thirties to develop film projects, he quickly
turned to the Prohibition era as one of the first stories he wanted to tell
on celluloid. This was a subject he knew very well. As a reporter and
columnist, he had become personally acquainted with many of the
eccentric and shady characters who had made the 1920s roar. To
encapsulate the decade, he focused on two of those acquaintances,
racketeer Larry Fay and nightclub hostess Texas Guinan. In fictionalized form, they became James Cagney and Gladys George on screen.

In *The Roaring Twenties*, Cagney's Eddie Bartlett is a World War I
veteran with one simple ambition upon his return to New York. He just
wants to reclaim his prewar job as an auto mechanic. But as hard times
settle over the country after the war, he is frustrated in his attempts to
resume his old life. Soon he gives in to temptation by trying out the
booming new business of selling illicit liquor. He makes it big in bootlegging, buys a swanky nightclub hosted by the tough-talking Panama
Smith (George), and becomes a leading underworld figure. He could
also become Panama's man if he wants to (she carries a torch for him),
but he is smitten by his club's young singer (Priscilla Lane) even though
she has no romantic interest in him. Eventually he loses his nightclub
and his fortune after the stock market crash of 1929 and his operations
are usurped by his former partner (Humphrey Bogart, in his early days
as an irredeemable heavy).

Cagney may be an innocent at the beginning of the film, but Larry
Fay, the real Eddie Bartlett, never was so pure. Still, as Thomas Coffey
points out in his book *The Long Thirst*, there was some Runyonesque
pathos about him. Although Fay never veered very far from the life of
crime, he desperately wanted to be considered legit and tried for most
of his life to use his streetwise cunning as a means of climbing the
social ladder.

A tough kid who grew up in Hell's Kitchen, Fay joined a street gang
as soon as he was big enough to hold his own. He ran up a sizable string
of minor arrests while still a teenager. Like Cagney, the actor, he came
from an Irish immigrant family but of a distinctly different physical
type. While the actor was a compact, well-proportioned bantamweight,
Fay measured six-foot-three and was lantern-jawed and gangly.

After winning a large bet at the racetrack, Fay flirted with working-class respectability by buying a taxicab. It did not take much to lead him astray. Soon after the Eighteenth Amendment initiated Prohibition, he set his sights on the huge profits that could be made transporting Canadian whiskey. Like Eddie Bartlett, he assembled a fleet of cabs and used them to deliver the illegal hooch.

As successful as the bootlegging business was, and even though he was willing to resort to strong-arm tactics when he felt it necessary, Fay did not relish the reputation that went with his thuggish station in life. To acquire some class, he put his money into creating a cabaret called the El Fey Club, his first of several nightspots. He pulled in a wealthy crowd with posh trappings, pretty showgirls, high prices, and the presence of the audacious hostess Texas Guinan, whom he lured away from a nearby speakeasy. Once, to his delight, Fay even ushered Lord and Lady Mountbatten into his club. He seemed to have arrived, perhaps even putting his Hell's Kitchen roots behind him. But not for long.

In the late 1920s, his veneer of class chipped away. Federal prosecutors padlocked his club for selling illicit booze and eventually forced him to close it down. For a while he ran a price-fixing and protection racket as head of a milk wholesalers' association, but an indictment squeezed him out of that as well. By the early 1930s, he had become a fallen star. He may not have stooped to being a hopeless drunk as Eddie Bartlett did in *The Roaring Twenties*, but he was a desperate hustler living on credit, eking out a living as a front man for a nightclub suffocating beneath the weight of the Great Depression. The end came on New Year's Day, 1932, a little under two years before the end of Prohibition. When bad times forced Fay to cut his doorman's pay, the employee channeled his frustration by cornering his boss inside the club and putting four bullets into him. Rather then staggering dramatically down the street, Fay simply flopped back onto a sofa, which just goes to show that some things are better left in the hands of filmmakers with some panache.

As it turns out, there doesn't seem to have been any drama of unrequited love between Larry Fay and Texas Guinan, as found in *The Roaring Twenties*. But in real life, Guinan didn't need any such sob-story prop to make her interesting. In fact, even though her fictional counter-part plays second fiddle to the Fay character in the Cagney film, Guinan was a more spectacular character than her racketeer boss.

Reared in Waco, Texas, she grew to larger-than-life proportions even as a young woman. She busted broncos, traveled with a Wild West show, and played the part of a cowgirl in two-reel westerns. Stints as a chorus girl and vaudeville performer followed before she discovered her greatest talent—setting the sort of breezy, devil-may-care tone that made Roaring Twenties crowds want to drink and cut loose.

Already middle-aged when Fay installed her as his official greeter and mistress of ceremonies, she no longer qualified as chorus-girl cute, but she definitely caught the eye. As described by Edmund Wilson, she was a "prodigious woman, with her pearls, her glittering bosom, her abundant beautifully bleached yellow coiffure, her formidable rap of white teeth, her broad bare back behind its grating of green velvet, the full-blown peony as big as a cabbage exploding on her broad green thigh." She welcomed customers by drawling "Hello, suckers" (in *The Roaring Twenties*, Gladys George substitutes the words, "Hello, chumps") and coined such memorable quips as, "Her brain is as good as new." Panama Smith was not the only thinly disguised portrait of Texas Guinan; the hostess was also awarded the ultimate Broadway honor by being fictionalized in Damon Runyon stories, under the intentionally recognizable moniker of Missouri Martin.

Guinan and Fay parted ways by the end of twenties, and like Fay, she fell on hard times as the roaring era came to a close. She tried unsuc-cessfully to open a club in France. She then managed to mount a revue back in America, but with the wild ways of the Jazz Age now in disfa-vor, a campaign for public decency put her show out of business. At her most desperate, she decided to jump to the other side of the fence and took a feeble stab at, of all things, barnstorming evangelism. She died of colitis on November 5, 1933, a month before voters repealed the Eighteenth Amendment. Like Fay, she was not quite able to get out of the Prohibition era alive.

A BUGGSY LIFE

Edward G. Robinson qualified as a true American original. On screen, he projected a personality that was completely unique. He was so memorably unique, in fact, that he was caricatured in a host of cartoons and impersonated by countless nightclub impressionists. No performance exemplified this distinctive quality more than his first starring role in the classic 1930 gangster movie *Little Caesar*. With his tommy-gun delivery of lines, his snarling intonations, and his stubby finger jabbing the air, he etched a vivid portrait that was all his own.

Or was it?

Not exactly. Or at least that's the assessment of certain aficionados of the Brooklyn underworld of the 1920s and 1930s. In his book *Tough Jews,* Rich Cohen writes, "Everyone familiar with the Brooklyn boys was convinced Edward G. Robinson based his film persona on Buggsy Goldstein, who had the same side-talking, duck-walking, tough-guy attitude as the movie star." Certainly a mere glance at a photo of Goldstein would suggest some sort of connection between the two men, almost as if there were some hushed-up familial relationship. The thick-lipped, toadlike Buggsy looks like he could easily have been Robinson's long-lost brother. If the actor did base many of his mannerisms on the Brooklyn hood, he chose his inspiration wisely. The street-tough persona, reconfigured into a number of variations, carried him through a long line of successful, entertaining films, from *The Last Gangster* and *A Slight Case of Murder* to *Key Largo* and *Hell on Frisco Bay*.

A mostly forgotten gangland figure, Buggsy Goldstein has been eclipsed in the public's memory by such mobster icons as Meyer Lansky, Lepke Buchalter, and Dutch Schultz. In his heyday, though, he was a force to be reckoned with—a deplorable force but still a force. As a teenager, he was known as a quiet kid, but crooks don't get tagged with a name like Buggsy for nothing—when angered he could fly into a murderous rage. With his

A BUGGSY LIFE

Brownsville, Brooklyn pal Abe "Kid Twist" Reles, he helped destroy the Shapiro mob and set up a new gang to control the territory. Big shots like Meyer Lansky and Lucky Luciano were impressed with the Brownsville boys' methods. They rewarded the boys by making them charter members of Murder, Inc., the Syndicate's kill-for-hire enforcement wing.

Eventually, one of Buggsy's contract hits caught up to him, thanks to his buddy Reles, who started squealing to the district attorney's office once he himself faced conviction on first-degree-murder charges. A jury convicted Goldstein and an icy piece of work named Pittsburgh Phil Strauss for the murder of a gambler named Puggy Feinstein. Goldstein and Strauss had killed Puggy in Reles's house. Strauss held the victim while Reles stabbed him with an ice pick. They all then started pummeling him until Puggy had the impertinence to bite Strauss's hand. Enraged, Strauss trussed up Puggy, connecting his limbs and neck with rope in such a way that the victim's thrashing-about caused his own slow strangulation. When it was all over, Buggsy, Strauss, and company drove the body to an open lot in Canarsie and set it ablaze.

Goldstein and Strauss died in the Sing Sing electric chair on June 12, 1941. If there's one thing that could be said in Goldstein's favor, it's that he didn't put on airs, like some self-important mobsters could. The other, better-known Bugsy of his time, Bugsy Siegel, would be offended if anyone dared call him by what he considered to be his demeaning nickname. Not Goldstein. If anyone asked his name, he would proudly say, "Buggsy." Being known as a crazy psychopath was no reason to be ashamed as far as he was concerned.

Rocky

This franchise-making boxing drama was inspired partly by the writer-star's own life. Before creating the *Rocky* screenplay, Sylvester Stallone was searching for a theme that would dramatize his experience at that time. A mostly unemployed actor, he was groping for that ever-elusive breakthrough that would get his career on track. He wanted to write about a character who struggled with that same sort of frustration and then eventually got the chance to turn his life around. But Stallone didn't discover the shape that the story would take until a night in March 1975 when he watched Muhammad Ali defend his heavyweight title on closed-circuit television.

Battling Ali that night was a little-known fighter named Chuck Wepner. More brawler than boxer, Wepner had compiled a winning record in and around his native New Jersey, but his opponents were generally unimpressive and he was not even a full-time pugilist. His days were spent working as a liquor salesman. Ali's handlers had selected him basically as a training exercise for the champ while he worked himself up to his next fight against a real contender like Joe Frazier or George Foreman. Wepner was supposed to be a pushover. But he did not quite cooperate. Somehow he stayed in the ring with the phenomenal Ali and lasted until the fifteenth round. His tenacity and courage inspired Stallone, who realized he had finally found the premise for his script. Having trained as a boxer as a teenager, he could easily imagine himself as a Wepner-like underdog who finally gets his chance for glory.

Like Rocky Balboa, Chuck Wepner fit the part of an ethnic working-class hero, although, unlike an ethnic thoroughbred like the Italian Stallion, Wepner was more of a mongrel—part Ukrainian, part Polish, and part German. While Rocky's home was Philadelphia, Wepner lived some seventy miles northwest of there in the New Jersey port of Bayonne. When he signed up for the match against Ali, he was already thirty-five years old. He had served in the marines, and had worked as a security guard and a nightclub bouncer. He was regarded as a club fighter, without a lot of pugilistic polish but willing to slug it out whenever called.

At six-foot-five and 220 pounds, he certainly looked like a heavyweight. He didn't have much of a jab, but his manager insisted he had a wicked right, and it was well known that he could take a punch. He also possessed an extraordinary talent for bleeding. In fight after fight, cuts around his eyes had opened up, requiring over three hundred stitches all told. In the words of *Sports Illustrated*'s Mark Kram, Wepner, the Bayonne Bleeder, was the type of fighter "who turns a ring into a red-wine sea."

According to fight-game observers, Wepner did not figure merely as an underdog in his upcoming match with Ali. He was a joke. As one wag put it, "After this one's over, he will be an object of art for the National Sewing Club." Least impressed of all was Ali. To show his contempt for Wepner, he refused to undergo a full-fledged training for the bout.

Wepner, meanwhile, was inspired by the opportunity of a lifetime. He was going to earn $100,000 for this fight, ten times more than any other purse in his career. And for the first time in his eleven years as a boxer, he was going to train full-time. Until then, preparation for a fight was something he had to confine to early mornings and nights, before and after his day job. Now he could whip himself into shape for an uninterrupted eight weeks at a Catskill Mountains training camp.

Although the experts remained skeptical, other less conventional observers were intrigued by Wepner's underdog appeal. Some offered devices to help the Bayonne brawler, from springs installed in the fighter's shoes that would improve his footwork to mysterious South Sea potions guaranteed to infuse him with special warrior's powers.

In the end, Wepner entered the ring in Cleveland with nothing but a soundly conditioned body and a fierce will to win. Ali came prepared to toy with him. Sometimes he taunted him with his lighter-than-air footwork, capering around the big lug, stinging him occasionally with lightning jabs just to show that he could strike at will. Other times he fell back on his rope-a-dope routine that he had made famous earlier that year during his momentous rumble-in-the-jungle with George Foreman. In the seventh round, to no one's great surprise, Ali opened a gash above Wepner's left eye. The bleeding began. Wepner plodded on. The eighth round came and went. The ninth round commenced. If Wepner's dogged persistence was starting to worry Ali, he didn't show it. Then Wepner landed a right to the chest.

A moment later Ali was sprawled on the canvas.

Somehow Wepner had done the inconceivable. Only three times before this fight had Ali been knocked down. Now the club fighter from Bayonne had delivered knockdown number four. Here was a turning-of-the-tables so dramatic that Stallone would incorporate the incident in his script, in the scene where Rocky drops the showboating Apollo Creed (an obvious Ali stand-in) with a crushing left to the head in the first round.

In actuality, Wepner's knockdown was not quite as earthshaking as it seemed. Ali claimed that he lost his balance because Wepner had stepped on one of his feet. Photographs seem to bear this out. Instead of rocking the champ, Wepner's punch only got him angry and forced him, finally, to take the challenger seriously. Even so, Ali's subsequent flurries of lefts and rights failed to put Wepner away as quickly as he might have expected. For six more rounds, the Bayonne Bleeder hung in there.

He nearly made it through the fifteenth and final round. Nineteen seconds before the concluding bell, Ali finished a barrage of punches with a devastating right cross that knocked Wepner off his feet and left him draped between the ropes, his face a pulpy, bloody mess. The referee declared Ali the winner. The champ, who had been so sure of an effortless victory, sank to the canvas, totally drained.

Like Rocky Balboa in the first sequel of Stallone's film series, Wepner was showered with media attention after his fight with the champion. From there on, though, the Balboa and Wepner stories diverge. The Bayonne Bleeder never got another title shot. Much worse, he let the fast times sweep him away as he developed a cocaine habit and eventually served a three-year stretch in prison for drug possession. Ironically, this detour from the *Rocky* pattern led to one more intersection between Wepner and Stallone. When the star was working on the prison movie *Lock Up*, the film company shot some scenes at New Jersey's Northern State Prison, where the onetime contender was incarcerated. Stallone asked to meet with Wepner. The star spent some time talking with him, and he let the film's cast and crew know that Wepner was the real Rocky.

Since leaving prison in 1991, Wepner has found work in the public relations field. In his spare time, the Bayonne Bleeder, who once inspired a struggling young actor, now takes on frequent engagements as a motivational speaker.

Rope

Released in 1948, *Rope* was Alfred Hitchcock's first color film, as well as his first with Jimmy Stewart, who was later to star in such 1950s Hitchcock classics as *The Man Who Knew Too Much*, *Rear Window*, and *Vertigo*. What really makes *Rope* distinctive, however, is the *way* it was filmed. The whole movie was shot in continuous, ten-minute takes which were then cleverly stitched together to provide the illusion of unbroken camera movement.

As a filmmaking experiment, *Rope* is still intriguing to watch. (It's especially fun to see the ingenious tricks Hitchcock devised to conceal the cuts between segments.) But even Hitchcock's virtuoso technique can't resolve the basic problem of the movie—namely, its flagrant staginess. Based on a play by Patrick Hamilton, the movie—confined to a single, penthouse set and taking place in "real time"—is an undeniably clever but overly theatrical piece that, in spite of the fluid camera work, has the static quality of a talky Broadway parlor mystery.

Even so, the film is energized by intense, compelling performances and moments of high suspense that are pure, vintage Hitchcock. The first few moments of the film deliver a powerful jolt. After focusing on a New York City street during the opening credits, the camera moves in through a curtained penthouse window, where a shocking murder is reaching its climax. A young man in dinner clothes is being brutally strangled by a pair of his mates, who proceed to stash his body in an antique living room chest.

We are quickly introduced to the killers: Brandon (John Dall), a haughty, brittle psychopath who fancies himself a Nietzschean superman, and his pretty-boy companion, Philip (Farley Granger), a quivering bundle of nerves who spends the whole movie teetering on the brink of hysteria. As the homicidal chums (and, by implication at least, gay lovers) discuss their crime, we learn that they have strangled the victim, their friend David Kentley, simply for the thrill of it—to prove that they are superior beings who can commit the perfect crime.

To add an extra dash of excitement to the proceedings, Philip has invited David's parents, fiancée, and a few mutual friends over for a dinner party that very night. Indeed, thoughout the movie, Philip (who is far and away the more perverse of the two thrill killers) is constantly dreaming up ways to make the experience as titillating as possible—even going so far as to serve the meal, buffet-style, atop the very chest in which David's corpse is stashed!

Tension builds as the evening proceeds. While David's family and friends grow increasingly concerned about his inexplicable absence, one of the guests—Rupert Kadell, Philip's former mentor at prep school—becomes more and more suspicious. In the end, Rupert—who had passed many late-night hours at prep school discussing Nietzschean concepts with Philip—realizes to his horror that the twisted young man has turned their philosophical musings into a justification for murder. After wrestling a revolver away from Brandon, he fires it through the apartment window. As sirens approach in the background, the three men sit down to await the arrival of the police.

The final credits of the film are followed by the standard disclaimer: "The characters and events depicted in this photoplay are fictitious. Any similarity to actual persons, living or dead, is purely coincidental." While it is true that the action of *Rope*—the macabre dinner party with the makeshift bier serving as a buffet table—is strictly make-believe, it is disingenuous to pretend that the main characters are equally fictitious. For there is nothing at all coincidental about the striking similarity between Brandon and Philip and the real-life Leopold and Loeb, the infamous teenage "thrill killers" of the 1920s.

The Leopold and Loeb case is a perfect example of the phenomenon the French call a *folie à deux*—a senseless crime committed by two closely joined people who, individually, would be incapable of conceiving, let alone carrying through, such a horrendous deed. Lifelong friends (and homosexual partners), Nathan Leopold and Richard Loeb were the scions of two prominent Jewish families residing in a posh Chicago suburb. Both boys were intellectual prodigies. At the time of their crime, the eighteen-year-old Loeb had already gotten his bachelor's degree from the University of Michigan and was doing graduate work at the University of Chicago. The nineteen-year-old Leopold— who had a genius-level IQ of 210—was fluent in five languages, taught private courses in ornithology, and planned to enroll in Harvard Law School later that year.

They were both also profoundly disturbed individuals. "Dickie" Loeb (the prototype for *Rope*'s Brandon) was a classic psychopath, outwardly polished and charming but utterly devoid of conscience, fellow feeling, or a capacity for remorse. He had committed assorted crimes, ranging from burglary to arson, from the time he was a child. In his fantasies, he was a criminal superman who exerted absolute power over a gang of worshipful subordinates. "Babe" Leopold (like the fictitious Philip, the more sympathetic of the pair) was in sexual thrall to his companion. In *his* fantasies (which dovetailed perfectly with Loeb's daydreams of Nietzschean dominance), he saw himself a slave who existed merely to make all the desires of his "king" come true.

Sometime in 1923, these brilliant but decidedly perverse companions began dreaming of committing the "perfect crime." On May 21, 1924, after seven months of preparation, they put their plan into effect. Selecting at random a fourteen-year-old acquaintance named Bobby Franks as he walked home from school, they lured him into their rented car, bludgeoned him with a chisel, shoved a gag down his throat, then drove his corpse to a remote marshy wasteland (familiar to Leopold from his bird-watching expeditions), where they poured hydrochloric acid on his face and penis, then stuffed his naked body into a drainpipe. Returning to Leopold's home, they put in a call to Bobby Franks's home and—pretending to be someone named "Johnson"—informed the horror-struck parents that their son had been kidnapped but would be returned unharmed upon the receipt of $10,000 in old twenty- and fifty-dollar bills. The next morning, before the ransom could be paid, a couple of railroad workmen stumbled upon a corpse, which was quickly identified as that of the missing Franks boy.

Though fancying themselves criminal masterminds who could get away with murder, the pair had actually committed a string of blunders that led, within a very short time, to their apprehension (among other slipups, Leopold had dropped his eyeglasses at the murder scene). With the arrest of the pampered young "thrill killers," the case became a nationwide sensation. The sheer, motiveless horror of their crime confirmed the country's worst fears about the immoral "flaming youth" of the period.

With the public clamoring for the young killers' execution and the Chicago DA out for their blood, Leopold and Loeb's millionnaire fathers hired the legendary lawyer Clarence Darrow to defend their sons. At the opening of the trial, Darrow shocked the court by pleading guilty. A passionate opponent of the death penalty, Darrow knew that his chances of persuading a jury to spare the lives of his clients was almost nil. By entering a guilty plea, he would have to convince only a single man—the presiding judge, John R. Claverly.

The "trial of the century," which began in July 1924, climaxed one month later with a stirring speech by Darrow, widely regarded as the finest of his fabled career. He spoke movingly of the bond between fathers and sons. He quoted A. E. Housman's poetry. He derided the prosecution for its blood lust and made a plea for "love and understanding" that moved the spectators to tears.

In the end, his eloquence triumphed. Leopold and Loeb were spared the gallows and sentenced to life in prison. Twelve years later, in January 1936, Loeb had his throat slit in the prison shower by his cellmate. Leopold won a parole in 1958, moved to Puerto Rico, earned a master's degree, married a doctor's widow, and wrote a book about birds. He died of a heart attack in 1971 at the age of sixty-six.

Since the release of *Rope*, there have been two other cinematic treatments of the Leopold and Loeb case: the thinly fictionalized 1954 thriller *Compulsion* and the somewhat mannered 1992 art film *Swoon*.

Saturday Night Fever

> "Everything described in this article is factual and was either witnessed by me or told to me directly by the people involved. Only the names of the main characters have been changed."
>
> —Nik Cohn, 1976
>
> "I faked it. I conjured up the story [of the main character] and named him Vincent . . . I made it all up. And presented it as fact . . . Bluntly put, I cheated."
>
> —Nik Cohn, 1997

In its June 7, 1976, issue, *New York* magazine ran a cover story by British writer Nik Cohn entitled "Tribal Rites of the New Saturday Night." The story—prefaced with a note from the author, declaring that "everything described in this article is factual"—was, in effect, a piece of pop, urban anthropology, a glimpse into the lifestyle of what Cohn described as a "whole new generation" of New Yorkers. Living in the outer boroughs of the city—Bronx, Brooklyn, Queens—these were "kids of sixteen to twenty, full of energy, urgency, hunger." Cut off from the chic world of Manhattan, they were the product of their economically hard-pressed time and place. Unlike the pampered flower children of the 1960s, these teens had come of age in an era of shortage. "So the new generation takes few risks," Cohn wrote. "It goes through high-school, obedient; graduates, looks for a job, saves and plans. And once a week, on Saturday night, its one great moment of release, it explodes."

The article focused on a single member of this new generation, who was meant to epitomize the whole. This was an eighteen-year-old Italian kid from Bay Ridge, Brooklyn, identified only as "Vincent." Owner of "fourteen floral shirts, five suits, eight pairs of shoes, three overcoats," Vincent sold paint in a neighborhood housewares store and shared an apartment with his mother and two younger sisters. (His father, a thief, was in jail; his second brother was in the hospital recuperating from a car crash; and his third brother had fled to Manhattan.) During the week, he led an existence of utter routine and drudgery. When Saturday night arrived, however, he and his pals—a group that called themselves "The Faces"—cut loose at whatever club was hot at the moment. At the time that Cohn studied them, their dance place of choice was the "2001 Odyssey" disco.

Vincent's evening would begin with his elaborate preparations. He would spend long periods of time regarding himself in the mirror: "Black hair and black eyes, olive skin, a slightly crooked mouth, and teeth so white, so dazzling, they always seemed fake." After arraying himself in his snappiest threads—"open-necked shirt, ablaze with reds and golds . . . Gucci-style loafers, complete with gilded buckle, and high black pants tight as sausage skins"— he'd saunter into the night, hook up with his buddies, and head for the disco. Inside the club—a "Saturday-night cathedral," where "music blared from the speakers [and] colored lights swirled back and forth across the dance floor"—Vincent was king. As he made his way to the center of the floor, the crowd would "fall back before him." Girls would run up to him, plant a kiss on his mouth, and exclaim, "Oooh, I just kissed Al Pacino." Others were content just to stand on the sidelines and watch him dance.

This was the moment when Vincent felt most alive. Commanding the floor—performing the Rope Hustle, or Bus Stop, or Odyssey Walk—he was a local legend, the best dancer in Bay Ridge, a homegrown superstar. At the same time, Vincent was aware that his dancing days couldn't last forever. At eighteen and a half, he was already feeling old.

Stuck in aimless, dead-end lives, Vincent and "The Faces"—Joey, Gus, John James, and Eugene, the 1970s version of a gang of fifties "JDs"—would relieve their frustrations through the usual means: i.e., sex and violence. Girls were divided into two categories. There were a few, rare specimens who—by dint of their unsullied reputations— might be lucky enough to be chosen by one of the Faces as his steady. In general, however, "the female function was simply to be available" at all times. Vincent himself had once been in love and even planned to get engaged. But after his girlfriend committed the cardinal sin of dancing with someone else, he found he "couldn't stand to touch her" anymore.

To alleviate their boredom, Vincent and his cohorts could also count on periodic run-ins with rival gang members. In one episode recounted by Cohn, the Faces plot revenge after their buddy John James is set upon by three Puerto Ricans and ends up in the hospital.

Tony Manero—the movie character based on Vincent and the role that made John Travolta a superstar—is a more appealing and sensitive figure than the one depicted in Cohn's article. And in other ways, too, *Saturday Night Fever* mitigates the harshness of Cohn's story by adding a bunch of typically Hollywood touches, from a tear-jerking suicide to a rousing brawl in an enemy hangout to the burgeoning relationship between Tony and his upwardly mobile partner, Stephanie. On the whole, however, the screenplay derives not only its main characters and overall atmosphere from Cohn's article but many of its incidents and details, from the "I just kissed Al Pacino" bit, to the attack on John James, to the protagonist's dead-end job as a paint salesman in a neighborhood housewares store.

To people familiar with the genesis of *Saturday Night Fever*, therefore, it came as a shock when, in December 1997—on the twentieth anniversary of the film—Nik Cohn published a retrospective piece in *New York* magazine in which he confessed that his famous, culture-changing story had been completely made up!

According to this second account, Cohn had initially encountered disco in the winter of 1975 when he visited a club in upstate New York and met a dancer nicknamed Tu Sweet. At the time, disco was still a subcultural fad that had started in gay black clubs and been picked up by a few local groups around New York City—Latinos in the Bronx, West Indians on Staten Island, and Italians in Brooklyn.

After receiving a lukewarm go-ahead from his editor—who, like most people, had never so much as *heard* of disco—Cohn made a field trip out to Bay Ridge with Tu Sweet as his guide. His research got off to a notably inauspicious start. As his cab drew up in front of the 2001 Odyssey club, he saw that a drunken brawl was under way. Just as he opened the car door, one of the participants staggered up and vomited all over Cohn's leg. He decided to call it a night. As the cab pulled away, however, Cohn looked through the window and saw something that would stick in his mind: "a figure in flared crimson pants and a black body shirt, standing in the club doorway, directly under the neon light and calmly watching the action. There was a certain style about him—an inner force, a hunger, and a sense of his own specialness."

Returning to the club the following weekend, Cohn searched for this compelling figure, but to no avail. In fact, the entire trip turned out to be an utter waste of time. "I didn't learn much . . . The noise level was deafening, the crush of sweaty bodies suffocating, and none of my attempts at conversations got beyond the first few sentences. Plus, I made a lousy interviewer. I knew nothing about this world, and it showed."

With nothing concrete to write about, Cohn made a fateful decision: "I faked it. I conjured up the story of the figure in the doorway, and named him Vincent . . . Then I went back to Bay Ridge in daylight and noted the major landmarks. I walked some streets, went into a couple of stores. Studied the clothes, the gestures, the walks. Imagined about how it would feel to burn up, all caged energies, with no outlet but the dance floor and the rituals of Saturday night. Finally, I wrote it all up. And presented it as fact."

Not long after "Tribal Rites of the New Saturday Night" hit the stands in June 1976, Cohn was contacted by movie producer Robert Stigwood, who managed the Bee Gees and had recently signed the young John Travolta to a movie deal. Stigwood thought that Cohn's Saturday-night story would translate into a perfect vehicle for the up-and-coming actor. The rest, as they say, is pop-culture history.

Cohn knew, of course, that—in passing off his fiction as fact—he was breaking the most fundamental rules of journalism. The knowledge, he claims, "came to eat me up." Still, he admits that he didn't feel bad enough to return any of the nice juicy checks he received over the years.

In the end, therefore, *Saturday Night Fever* represents an unusual, perhaps unique, case in the annals of "real-to-reel" movies: a fictional film based on an ostensibly factual story that turned out, in the end, to be pure make-believe.

Saving Private Ryan

> "It's not a biography of our family, but
> the parallels are amazing."
>
> —Cate Niland Remme

Since artists pride themselves on their originality, they are sometimes reluctant to admit that they have gotten their ideas from real-
life sources—that their creations didn't spring entirely from their own
imaginations. Horror novelist Robert Bloch, for example—the author
of *Psycho*—consistently downplayed the extent to which his character,
Norman Bates, was based on the notorious Wisconsin ghoul, Ed Gein.
And in spite of the obvious parallels, Captain Frank Mundus—the so-
called Montauk Monster Man—has never been explicitly acknowledged as the model for the shark-hating Quint of *Jaws*.

As it happens, *Jaws* isn't the only Steven Spielberg blockbuster
whose apparent true-life inspiration has been played down (and even
explicitly denied) by its creators. The same situation applies to his harrowing, widely hailed combat film *Saving Private Ryan*. Set during the
D-day invasion and its immediate aftermath, the movie centers on an
eight-man squad led by Captain John Miller (Tom Hanks). After surviving the horrors of the landing on Omaha Beach, Miller and his men are
sent on a perilous mission behind enemy lines to locate and rescue a

young paratrooper James Ryan (Matt Damon), whose three brothers have been killed in action. Though Spielberg and his collaborators have insisted that the screenplay is entirely fictional, few commentators have failed to note its remarkable resemblance to the tragic true-life story of Sergent Frederick "Fritz" Niland, as recounted in the 1992 book *Band of Brothers* by World War II historian Stephen Ambrose (who was made an ex post facto consultant on the film after it was already completed).

Born in the upstate New York town of Tonawanda, just outside of Buffalo, Fritz Niland was the youngest of six children, four boys and two girls. Their father, Mike, a steel-mill manager, had fought in the Spanish-American War as one of Teddy Roosevelt's celebrated Rough Riders. When America declared war on Japan in 1941 following the attack on Pearl Harbor, Fritz's three older brothers—following in the proud military footsteps of the elder Niland—immediately signed up for service. Edward, twenty-eight, became an army-air-corps gunner; Preston, twenty-six, a paratrooper; and Robert, twenty-two, a mortar gunner.

Eager to follow his brothers' lead, Fritz joined the army and eventually found himself taking part in the D-day invasion as a member of Easy Company, 506th Parachute Infantry Regiment, 101st Airborne Division. A week later, with the liberation of France well under way, Niland learned that his brother Bob had been killed on D-day while manning a machine gun against an encircling force of Germans. Heartbroken by the news, Fritz hitched a ride to see another brother, Preston, a platoon leader in the 4th Infantry Division—only to discover that Preston, too, had been killed on D-day, on Utah Beach.

The final blow came when Fritz returned to Easy Company and found the chaplain, Father Francis Sampson, waiting for him with devastating news: the oldest of the Niland brothers, Edward, a pilot in the China-Burma-India theater, was missing in action and presumed dead.

As awful as this triple tragedy was for Fritz, it must have been even more agonizing for his mother, Augusta, who (like her fictional counterpart in *Saving Private Ryan*) received all three official telegrams informing her of her losses on the same day.

A month after D-day, the remnants of Easy Company were evacuated to England for a week of R&R before a forthcoming assault on Holland. On July 13, Fritz Niland was sitting in his barracks, lamenting the loss of two thirds of his outfit during the Normandy invasion, when Father Sampson appeared. The chaplain, it turned out, was there to tell him that—in keeping with military policy that no family should suffer the death of more than two sons—the army was withdrawing Fritz Niland from the combat zone and sending him back to the States.

When Niland protested—"No, I'm staying here with my boys"— Father Sampson informed him that he could take the matter up with General Eisenhower or President Roosevelt. But, in the meantime, Sergeant Niland was going home.

There are, of course, important differences between the real-life Niland case and the fictional story of Private James Ryan. For one thing, it turned out that the eldest of the Niland brothers, Edward, didn't die in combat after all. Having survived the downing of his B-25 bomber over Burma, Edward ended up in a Japanese prison camp. Though he lost seventy pounds during his torturous ordeal as a POW, he eventually managed to escape and was rescued by British troops. He died in 1984—outliving Fritz by a year.

Moreover, there were other families who suffered equally terrible losses. As Stephen Ambrose notes, "there were probably hundreds of cases of multiple brothers being killed in the war." Perhaps the most famous of these tragedies involved the Sullivans, five Irish-American brothers from Iowa who all perished at sea when their ship, the U.S.S. *Juneau,* was sunk in 1942. As a result of this tragedy, the War Department adopted the so-called Sullivan Law, which sought to prevent such future catastrophes by barring brothers from serving in the same unit. (Fifty-four years before *Saving Private Ryan*, Hollywood paid tribute to this staggering familial sacrifice in the patriotic drama *The Fighting Sullivans*.)

Still, as one commentator has written, the connections between Spielberg's film and the story of the Niland family are "inescapable." In apparent acknowledgment of this fact, Fritz Niland's surviving family members were invited to the Hollywood premiere of *Saving Private*

Ryan and given red-carpet treatment—hotel rooms, limo service, etc. After viewing the film, Fritz's daughter, Cate Remme, offered what is perhaps the definitive comment on Spielberg's epic and the true-life drama it so strikingly rsembles.

"It is not a biography of our family," she observed. "But the parallels are amazing."

FATHERLY INSPIRATION

The title character of *The Great Santini* is easily one of the more vivid film protagonists in recent years, alternately colorful, outlandish, and frightening. Bull Meechum, who adopts the Great Santini nickname as a tribute to his virtuoso ability as a fighter pilot, is a lifelong marine who never seems to stop waging war, even when home during peacetime. He is considered an endearing maverick at marine bases, where upending a pal and sticking his head in the toilet is considered a scampish prank. But at home he is a wildly unpredictable tyrant. He addresses his children as if they were boot-camp recruits, commands his son to punch out an opponent during a high-school basketball game, and batters his wife while on drunken binges. Whatever else he may be, Bull Meechum (as portrayed by a strutting, intense Robert Duvall) is truly unforgettable.

The source for the character and the film was an early Pat Conroy novel, published in 1976. When the author went on book-signing junkets, he was often accompanied by his father, who felt, quite rightly, that he deserved some credit for the novel's success. Without him the book would not have been written—and the novelist's early home life would have been much less agonizing. Colonel Donald Conroy was, in fact, the real Great Santini, even sporting the same nickname, which he had borrowed from a magician that he had seen as a child.

Like Meechum, Colonel Conroy was a genuine marine hero. A profes-

(continued ...)

Fatherly Inspiration

sional soldier whose combat experience spanned thirty years, he flew missions in World War II, the Korean War, and in Vietnam. And he was as consumed with flamboyant bravado as his son's fictional creation. He once claimed that the Russians backed down during the Cuban missile crisis because they heard that he had been posted as squadron commander in nearby Puerto Rico.

At home, Conroy was remembered more as a great terror than as a magical warrior. His four sons bore the brunt of his rages, which could become so fierce that on at least one occasion a Conroy boy had to be taken to the hospital emergency ward. When his cruelty and brutality were exposed in his son's novel, Colonel Conroy wasn't quite sure how to characterize the book's relation to reality. On the one hand, he denied that he had been guilty of the offenses described by his son, but egotist that he was, he was also eager to bask in the media glow that came with being identified as the real-life inspiration for the book.

One thing that the novel accomplished: it proved that sometimes literature can shape reality for the better. Soon after *The Great Santini*'s publication, the real Santini turned over a new leaf. Whether he truly underwent a change of heart or was merely burnishing his image for the public's consumption, Colonel Conroy began acting like a kind, caring parent for the first time. Years later, just before Colonel Conroy died of cancer in 1998, *The Great Santini* author Pat Conroy was always close at hand during his father's final illness.

Six Degrees of Separation

In this 1993 adaptation of John Guare's play, a young man shows up at an upper-crust Manhattan apartment inhabited by a couple who are complete strangers to him. Within hours, he acquires a free meal, a bed for the night, and a fifty-dollar handout. He first manages to get through the door by pretending to be a mugging victim. From there he goes on to claim that he is a college friend of the apartment owners' children, then proceeds to pass himself off as the son of Sidney Poitier. It is an exhibition of remarkable brazenness, a virtuoso feat of lying. And it's all essentially true, based on a real event.

Guare, a Manhattanite himself, first heard about the real-life con job from friends of his who had been duped by the impostor. This was in 1983, immediately after the event. At first, the playwright didn't pay much attention to the anecdote. Then, six years later, after the story had simmered in his mind, he came upon old newspaper articles about the case, and the idea for the play began to take shape. The story of a facile young man who insinuates himself into strangers' lives became a vehicle for a comedy-drama about the insecurities of New York City life. By the time the play emerged as a hit in 1990, the man who had presented himself as "David Poitier" had already been in and out of prison for his scam. He did not, however, seem to grasp that he had done anything wrong.

The real name of the would-be "David Poiter" is David Hampton. While the con man in *Six Degrees of Separation* (played by Will Smith) starts out as a lowly street person, Hampton, as was revealed in Jeanie Kasindorf's *New York* magazine profile, grew up in comfort, the son of a successful Buffalo, New York, attorney. At seventeen, he left home for New York City, where he became, as he later put it, "a brilliant boy-about-town," although exactly in what way he was brilliant is not clear. He drifted for a while, spending some time back in Buffalo, taking some acting classes at the state university there. He began to wear out his welcome when he got himself arrested for stealing money from a student's dorm room.

Back in New York City in 1983, he refined his talent for securing free room and board. At first, while hanging around Columbia University, he presented himself as the friend of a campus gay-rights leader. This ruse got him into dorm rooms for the night, but more luxurious digs, which would be more to Hampton's liking, required a more glamorous facade. He proved he could take a crucial step up the social scale when he showed up one night at the apartment of Melanie Griffith, occupied at the time by fellow actor Gary Sinise. Here, Hampton developed a modus operandi that capitalized both on the prestige of a star's name and the classic hard-luck scam. Using his son-of-Poitier guise, he told Sinise that his plane for Los Angeles had left without him, but not without his money and luggage. Since, Hampton claimed, he was a friend of Melanie Griffith, he thought he'd come to her home for help. The result was a night in the fashionable apartment and a ten-dollar loan from Sinise. Obviously, Hampton was onto something.

He added another wrinkle to his technique when his wanderings took him to Connecticut College. He got a hold of a student's address book that supplied information on several graduates from the prestigious Andover prep school. He could now target the well-to-do parents of these students and then craft a double impersonation, purporting to be both the son of a movie star and a friend of their children.

Hampton's next foray into New York City would serve as the basis for *Six Degrees of Separation*, both on stage and on screen. The first Andover contacts he made were Jay and Lea Iselin (fictionalized into the characters played by Bruce Davison and Mary Beth Hurt in the film). Jay, at the time, was president of WNET, New York's public television station, and Lea was a lawyer. When Hampton phoned and told them his story about being mugged, the Iselins graciously extended an invitation to "David Poitier," supposed friend of their daughter. Later, in the middle of the night, the Iselins were wakened by the sounds of some sort of scuffle. Hampton told them a burglar had entered the apartment, but not to worry, he had driven him out. The Iselins suspected that their guest was not telling the truth. They told Hampton he had to leave first thing in the morning.

Two days later, Hampton worked the same hustle on Osborn and Inger Elliott (recast on film as the characters played by Donald Sutherland and Stockard Channing). Another prestigious host, Osborn Elliott was a Columbia University dean. Over dinner, Hampton held forth about his father's—Poitier's—plans to direct a film version of the musical *Dreamgirls* (in the film, the project is a filmization of *Cats*). This time, there was no commotion in the dead of night to rouse the hosts. Instead, Inger Elliott went into Hampton's room in the morning to wake him up, per his instructions, only to find Hampton in bed with another young man. (The "burglar" at the Iselin apartment may have been another of Hampton's companions.) In the play and film, Guare dramatizes the situation by having the con man's friend running stark naked through the apartment, upending furniture and making threats. In reality's milder version, Hampton came up with a punch line that actually topped these manufactured theatrics. When discovered in bed with his friend, he said, by way of explanation, that his bedmate was Malcolm Forbes's nephew. The Elliotts were not terribly impressed. Once again, Hampton was ejected from his hosts' premises.

The Elliotts and the Iselins were friends, and after comparing notes on their experiences with the suspicious David Poitier, they decided to contact the police. The arrest of the Will Smith character in *Six Degrees* closely parallels the capture of David Hampton. As in the film, the con man was arrested in the West Village after calling one of the women he had flimflammed.

At the end of Guare's fictionalized story, it's not clear whether the con artist will continue his fraudulent ways or turn over a new leaf. In real life, Hampton quickly left no doubt which direction he would take. After serving twenty-one months in prison, he returned to New York and soon was banned from the New York University campus. It seems Hampton was going around telling NYU students that he was the author of *Six Degrees of Separation*. He tried to parlay this spurious connection to show business into a place to stay for the night.

Smooth Talk

Connie (played by Laura Dern) is a high-school girl who is teetering on the edge of sexual awakening. At home, she can no longer be the little girl her father seems to think she is; she is unable to relate to her straitlaced older sister; and she is either unable or unwilling to live up to her beleaguered mother's expectations. As the family tensions fester, she ventures out to test her coltish sexual allure. With her friends, she makes herself up and parades herself through the local mall, the multiplex, and, finally, a neon-splashed burgers-and-beer joint, a known pickup spot. She goes out parking with some of the boys but finds she is unnerved by anything more than adolescent necking. What she doesn't know—and what is not revealed until the film's final scenes—is that a mysterious cruiser by the name of Arnold Friend (Treat Williams) has been keeping tabs on her.

Arnold, obviously older than Connie and her friends, carries himself with a strange, self-styled charisma. Accompanying him is a brooding, unsettling friend. Arnold comes to Connie's house one Sunday afternoon when her family is away and declares that he was meant to be her lover. Arnold fascinates her with his intensely low-keyed spiels on ardor and destiny. He also frightens her—although it's not spelled out, there is the sense that he is capable of dark deeds. Finally, though, Arnold succeeds in seducing her. The film ends in a disturbingly vague fashion. It's not clear what Arnold will do next and what he would resort to if things do not go his way.

This understated, mesmerizing little 1985 film is based on a short story by Joyce Carol Oates entitled "Where Are You Going, Where Have You Been?" The story on film comes across as a sort of modern Grimms fairy tale, dealing as it does with a young person turning away from her home and stumbling into a predicament thanks to a wicked spellbinder. The story is also reminiscent of a series of events that took place in Arizona in the mid 1960s. Evoking fairy tales once again, this real story revolved around a strange young man named Charles Schmid, who became known in the tabloid press as the Pied Piper of Tucson. But, unlike viewers of *Smooth Talk*, the people of Schmid's hometown did not have to imagine what their Arnold Friend–type figure was capable of. When he was through, Schmid left three teenage girls buried in the desert.

Charles Schmid was a short young man, measuring only five feet three inches in height, but he was determined to stand tall in the eyes of younger Tucson kids, both male and female. After high school, he recast himself as a magnetic, hipster figure, or at least his conception of what that might be. He dyed his hair jet-black and swept it up and back, like Elvis Presley. He wore cosmetics to perfect his complexion. He affixed a nasty-looking fake mole on his face to give himself a meaner appearance. His compact, gymnast's stature was something else he wanted to change. To make himself look taller, he layered paper inside his boots; sometimes he inserted crushed beer cans. This may have added an inch or two to his apparent height, but it also made it more difficult for him to walk. (Oates alludes to this habit in her story, when Connie notices Arnold's wobbly gait and surmises that his boots are stuffed with some sort of makeshift lifts.)

To complement his manufactured look, he adopted a roguish manner and a stream of verbal riffs crafted to capture the imagination of disaffected high-school kids. The older Schmid partied with booze and drugs, dabbled in the occult, and told extravagant tales about himself.

That staggering walk of his, for instance, had nothing to do with desperate attempts to increase his height. It had to do with an injury, he said, sustained while brawling one day with mobsters.

The following that these antics attracted proved that Schmid understood his audience. Teenage boys regarded the twenty-year-old as their leader. Teenage girls were at his beck and call, willing both to sleep with him and give him their money. Schmid acquired a sort of personal cult, a pre-flower-child version of Charles Manson and his Family. As Oates's story suggests, he knew how to single out potential disciples, then enchant them with a spell of words.

The sex, drugs, and rock and roll were enough to satisfy Schmid for a while, but then in the spring of 1964 he grew restless and wanted to raise the ante. One night he was getting drunk with two of his followers, Mary French and John Saunders, when he announced that he wanted to kill a girl. "I think I can get away with it," he said. The other two didn't need much persuading. They helped Schmid lure a fifteen-year-old named Alleen Rowe out of her house, then they all drove out to the desert. There Schmid raped the girl and smashed in her skull with a heavy rock.

Schmid's boast proved good for over a year—he did seem to get away with the thrill killing. Impressed with his senseless homicidal success, he decided to kill again late in the summer of 1965. Gretchen Fritz, a seventeen-year-old girlfriend, started to get too possessive. She also may have exacerbated the situation by trying to make Schmid jealous with stories that she had recently had a sexual fling while on a trip to California. One night in August, Schmid came upon Gretchen and her thirteen-year-old sister at a drive-in movie. Later that night he strangled them both and dumped them in the desert.

Committing the double murder was not enough for Schmid. Not forgetting his position as a juvenile ringleader, he wanted to share the experience with his friends. Over the next few months he told several of them about the killings and even took one of them out to give him a look at the Fritz girls' bodies decomposing in a ditch. This friend's name was Richard Bruns. He was not as favorably impressed by Schmid's insane behavior as others apparently were. After brooding for three months over what he had seen, Bruns called the police and tipped them off about Schmid's murder spree.

Schmid was given the death penalty but was fortunate enough to stall his execution with appeals until 1971 when the Supreme Court abolished capital punishment. His sentence was commuted to life imprisonment. Although he had succeeded in dazzling high-school kids in Tucson, Schmid's teen-idol persona was not likely to go over as well in prison. It's not clear whether he was able to invent a new routine for himself that was better suited to the sensibilities of hardened convicts. What we do know is that at least one inmate was not terribly taken with the Pied Piper of Tucson. At the end of a prison fight on March 20, 1975, guards found Schmid mortally wounded. One or more of his fellow convicts had stabbed him twenty times.

State of Grace

Set in Manhattan during the late 1970s—when gentrificaton was transforming the tough west-side neighborhood known as "Hell's Kitchen" into a Yuppie enclave renamed "Clinton"—Phil Joanou's *State of Grace* is a dark, violent gangster saga that begins like an Irish *Goodfellas* and ends like an urban *Wild Bunch*. Ed Harris turns in a typically intense performance as Frankie Flynn, the Irish mob boss who rules his home turf with terror while leading a respectable, middle-class life in the suburbs of New Jersey. Utterly ruthless and ferociously ambitious, Frankie has been attempting to solidify his power by joining forces with the "big boys"—the Italian Mafia.

Unfortunately, he is loaded down with a particularly heavy burden— his kid brother, Jackie (Gary Oldman), a stringy-haired, trigger-happy psycho whose idea of a really funny gag is to tickle someone with the chopped-off hands of a dismembered murder victim. Though possessed of a frighteningly violent temper, Jackie has a genuine soft spot in his heart for the old neighborhood and bitterly disapproves of his brother's attempts to cozy up to the Cosa Nostra.

At the center of the plot is Jackie's former best friend, Terry Noonan (Sean Penn), who shows up in his old haunts after a long, unexplained

208 ■ FOR REEL

absence. Though Terry tells his old pals that he has been leading a peri-
patetic existence, first as a marine down in Texas, then as a worker in
such exotic locales as Oklahoma and Milwaukee, the truth is very different. Having fled the mean streets of Hell's Kitchen for a more law-
abiding life in Boston, he has become a cop. Now he has returned to the
old neighborhood as an undercover agent. His assignment is to infil-
trate the Irish mob and gather enough evidence to bring down Frankie
Flynn.

Before long, however, Terry's affection for his old friends—who
include his former girlfriend, Kathleen (Robin Wright), the Flynn brothers' winsome sister—causes him to undergo a serious crisis of conscience. Torn between his commitment to the law and his feelings for
the people he grew up with, he becomes increasingly immobilized with
guilt. In the end, however—after Frankie commits the ultimate act of
treachery—Terry takes on the entire Flynn gang in a gun-blazing showdown in a neighborhood bar.

As a work of pure pop entertainment, *State of Grace* is filled with the
standard Hollywood ingredients, including steamy sex scenes between
Sean Penn and his future wife, Robin Wright; an intensely suspenseful
sequence in which Jackie and his heavily armed goons come close to
setting off a gangland apocalypse; and the prolonged, climactic gun battle—a balletic, slo-mo massacre straight out of a Sam Peckinpah movie.
For all its formulaic elements, however, Joanou's film does an effective
job of encapsulating the actual true-life case of the infamous New York
City gang known as the Westies, whose blood-drenched history is powerfully told by writer T. J. English in his 1990 book, *The Westies: Inside
the Hell's Kitchen Irish Mob.*

As English points out, the Westies were carrying on a criminal tradi-
tion dating back to the turn of the century, when Hell's Kitchen was
home to a variety of Irish street gangs like Parlor Mobs, the Gorillas,
the Tenth Avenue Gang, and the Gophers. During the post–World War II
era, the criminal kingpin of the area was a racketeer named Michael
"Mickey" Spillane. A handsome gentleman-gangster who favored thou-
sand-dollar suits and had powerful connections in the city's power
structure, Spillane ruled over his domain like an old-world Mafia don,

holding court in a Tenth Avenue tavern, doling out charity to the neighborhood needy, and enforcing his will with a judicious application of violence. In short, he was the Irish equivalent of an old-fashioned Sicilian "Man of Respect."

The late 1960s, however, gave rise to a new breed of Hell's Kitchen gangster who *lacked* all respect. In a dark reflection of the generational conflict roiling the country at large, a group of reckless young toughs appeared who regarded Spillane and his followers as a bunch of old fogies and sought to supplant them. Their leader was an utterly ruthless, wildly ambitious young man named Jimmy Coonan. Launching a violent war against Spillane, Coonan (the real-life prototype for the Frankie Flynn character in *State of Grace*) aspired to be the leader of the most feared and powerful gang in the whole, bloody history of Hell's Kitchen. By the mid-1970s, he had accomplished his dream.

What differentiated Coonan and his gang from their predecessors was a propensity for utterly savage violence. Enemies, real or perceived, would be murdered without hesitation, then made to do "the Houdini act," their corpses cut up with butcher knives, stuffed into garbage bags, and dumped into the East River. Indeed, the Westies' fondness for dismemberment quickly earned them a citywide notoriety. On one infamous occasion, Coonan's thirteen-year-old niece discovered him with a bagged, decapitated head in his arms. On another, he left his victim's castrated genitals in a milk carton as a joke. And in an incident echoed in the movie, he once stored a dead man's chopped-off hands in a freezer, intending to plant the fingerprints on a weapon at some later date.

Coonan's main crony in all this mayhem was his boyhood pal, Francis Thomas "Mickey" Featherstone, a small, baby-faced, deeply unstable Vietnam vet, subject to uncontrollable bouts of violence. Different aspects of the deeply conflicted Featherstone are embodied in the two fictitious characters played by Gary Oldman and Sean Penn. Like Oldman's Jackie Flynn, Featherstone was a frighteningly loose cannon whose criminal record included three homicides by the time he was twenty-two. With the feared Featherstone as his enforcer, Coonan quickly found himself as the undisputed head of the Hell's Kitchen rackets. In the end, however, it was Featherstone who (like Sean Penn's character, Terry Noonan) brought the Westies down.

What ultimately led to their undoing was Coonan's infatuation with the Italian mob. By the late 1970s, Coonan (like Frankie Flynn in the movie) was living with his family in an affluent New Jersey suburb. His criminal ambitions had not diminished, however. On the contrary. Aspiring to extend his racketeering beyond the bounds of Hell's Kitchen, he began to forge links with the Gambino crime family. His new alliance with the Mafia made Coonan an even more intimidating force in the New York underworld. Even when the feds nailed him on a gun possession charge, he continued to control his organization from behind bars.

At the same time that Coonan was in prison, Mickey Featherstone was doing time in a federal penitentiary. According to time-honored underworld traditions, his wife and children should have been well taken care of by the other gang members while Mickey was out of commission. Much to his dismay, however, his family's pleas for financial support were rebuffed. When he emerged from prison in 1983, his bitterness was compounded by Coonan's deepening ties to the Italian mob. In Mickey's view, his old friend seemed intent on selling out the neighborhood rackets to the "guineas."

The breaking point for Mickey Featherstone came in 1986, when he was convicted of the murder of a man named Michael Holly. Ironically (given how many homicides he had actually gotten away with), he was innocent of this one. Faced with a life sentence, filled with bitterness toward Coonan and a deep sense of betrayal, Mickey decided to turn informant. By the time he'd finished talking, he'd given the government information on no less than thirty unsolved murders, plus hundreds of violent assaults—to say nothing of the Irish mob's countless racketeering schemes. In March 1987, Rudolph Giuliani, the U.S. attorney for the Southern District of New York (and future mayor of the Big Apple), indicted Coonan and nine other gang members on fourteen counts, encompassing murder, loan sharking, extortion, counterfeiting, and income tax evasion.

In *State of Grace*, the Westies are obliterated in a prolonged, climactic bloodbath. The reality was much less explosive, though—in its own way—every bit as dramatic. With Mickey Featherstone spilling his guts on the stand (and the local tabloids playing up every lurid revelation for all it was worth), the defendants were convicted on all counts. Coonan was sentenced to seventy-five years without parole at Leavenworth. Featherstone and his family vanished into the Witness Protection Program. And the Westies—"the most savage organization in the long history of New York City gangs," in Giuliani's words—were history.

The Sting

Con men are a charming bunch of people—at least, they are on the movie screen. In real life, we may regard them as snakes in the grass, the lowest form of cheat. But while under the spell of a deft cinematic caper, we're more likely to see them as ingenious, disarming rogues, from slicksters like Ryan O'Neal in *Paper Moon* and James Garner in *The Skin Game* to the buffoonish Zero Mostel and Gene Wilder in *The Producers*. The star-powered grifters in *The Sting* are perhaps the most clever and engaging of all.

In this 1973 Oscar winner, Paul Newman and Robert Redford win our sympathy right from the beginning by setting their larcenous sights on a mark who clearly deserves to be taken: the vicious racketeer Robert Shaw, who, in the opening scenes, arranges the murder of Redford's friend and mentor. From there they proceed to divert us with one of the most elaborately orchestrated and finely tuned scams ever portrayed on film. For crafting this enjoyably tricky tale, screenwriter David S. Ward won an Academy Award, and his skill in unfolding all the story's twists and turns certainly deserved recognition. But to some extent the credit for the ingenuity of Newman and Redford's scheme belongs to the men who actually put over this sort of swindle in real life.

The name of Newman's character provides an obvious clue to the true-life inspiration for *The Sting*. The on-screen scammer is known as Henry Gondorff, a name that would certainly have rung a bell with denizens of the criminal underworld in the early 1900s. At that time, every self-respecting New York grifter would have heard of Charley and Fred Gondorf (spelled with one "f" instead of two), considered to be the most artful of con artists, veritable Michelangelos of the large-scale swindle. The big con featured in *The Sting* was patterned after a type of scheme considered to be the Gondorfs' masterpiece.

Like other successful businessmen, Charley and his younger brother Fred rose to the top of their profession by thinking big and by paying meticulous attention to the smallest of details. Paying off the police to look the other way didn't hurt either. Beginning in the 1870s, they applied themselves to a variety of enterprises, from rigged poker games to the selling of bogus stocks. Through it all, the Gondorfs cultivated a shrewd understanding of human nature, or at least, a particular avaricious sector of it. If they had ever boiled down their business philosophy to a single sentence, it probably would have been the classic line "You can't cheat an honest man." They may not have been charismatically handsome like their fictional counterparts in *The Sting*, and they may have been totally devoid of scruples, but at least it can be said that they targeted people who were themselves motivated by greed. The Gondorfs' schemes capitalized on their marks' desire to make easy, often ill-gotten, money.

The Gondorf technique reached its apex in a scam known as "the big store" or "the wire." The idea was to lure the sucker to a phony betting parlor where he would supposedly place a can't-miss bet on the races. Typically, the Gondorfs would claim to have a confederate at Western Union who was tapping into the telegraphed race results. This advance information would be relayed, the Gondorfs promised, to the mark, who would then put down a wager before the betting parlor itself got the results. Of course, the Gondorfs did not necessarily need an inside man at Western Union to stage this scene. They could simply run a race wire to their specially set-up betting room and then delay announcing the results, as is done in *The Sting*. In this way, the grifters could arrange for the mark to win, in order to prove that they could produce results, or set him up for a loss, when the time came to take the sucker's money. True artists that they were, the Gondorfs could spin several nimble variations on this big-store theme.

The particular scam that we know the most about occurred in 1914 and was engineered primarily by Charley. The pigeon, rather than an Irish racketeer as in *The Sting*, was a visiting Englishman. Named Eugene Adams, he was crossing the Atlantic on a steamship when he struck up a friendship with a fellow passenger named Potter. Or, rather, Potter struck up the friendship with him. Potter's real name was Jim Ryan, and he was an associate of the Gondorfs on the lookout for a likely target. Adams seemed to fit the bill. He was rich, he liked to gamble, and he didn't seem too fussy about taking advantage of privileged information. When the ship docked in New York on Saturday, July 25, Potter/Ryan took Adams to a café where he introduced the Englishman to Charley Gondorf. Gondorf claimed to be the man who handled bets for both the Vanderbilts and Astors. Adams was impressed. When Gondorf offered to take the Englishman to his betting room on West Forty-ninth Street, Adams readily agreed.

Ryan bet along with Adams, to put the mark at ease while they lost their first wager. Ryan then promised to make it up to Adams by consulting his ally at Western Union. When their next bet paid off, Adams became confident in his companion's tips and was ready to plunk down some big money—$10,000 worth. The money, though, took the form of a check. Undaunted, Gondorf let Adams win, to the tune of $135,000—but with one small proviso. Taking the Englishman into his office, Gondorf showed him the $135,000 in cash on his desk—in any case, it *looked* like real money—and said that the cash was Adams's as soon as the Englishman produced the $10,000 bet in cash. It was merely a formality, Gondorf assured him, just a matter of club policy and good faith. As a matter of fact, Gondorf went on, Adams could come back on

Monday and simply *show* the cash. He didn't even have to hand it over. Adams, eager to rake in his winnings, agreed to go along with the procedure.

On Monday, Adams arrived at the betting room to find his money waiting for him in a bag. He took his cash out of his pocket—playing slick himself, he actually produced only $4,500 instead of $10,000—and then, just at that moment, somebody banged loudly on the front door. The police were raiding the joint. Everyone scrambled to escape out the side door. In the confusion, Adams managed to grab his bag of winnings. At the same time, a Gondorf accomplice named Carbonelli grabbed Adams's $4,500 and took off. Naturally, when Adams got around to looking inside his bag, he found only cut paper. And the police raiders, of course, were actually Gondorf-hired impostors.

The Sting makes use of the Gondorfs' police-raid ploy at the climax of its big con, but then it borrows a trick from other big-store operators when Newman pretends to gun down Redford, thus adding to the dire pandemonium of the scene. This technique was perfected around the turn of the century by a grifter named Buck Boatright. To stage the supposedly fatal falling-out, the shooter fired blanks and the victim bit on a small pouch of chicken blood to unleash a stream of blood from his mouth. (In *The Sting*, we see Redford insert something in his mouth prior to the scam's final act, presumably to produce the same effect.)

Gondorf's big con of July 1914 differed from the Newman/Redford sting in two important ways. One, Gondorf was not acting out of justifiable revenge, merely out of avarice. And two, he got caught. Usually, when pulling off this kind of scam, he depended on the mark keeping quiet. After all, the sucker was involved in a shady deal himself and wouldn't care to tell the authorities about it. Adams, though, immediately went to the police, and two of Gondorf's men were apprehended the same day. Gondorf thought he could persuade Adams not to testify against his accomplices by giving him back the $4,500. A meeting for the payoff was set up, but detectives lurked nearby and pounced on Gondorf as soon as he handed over the money.

Charley Gondorf ended up serving time in Sing Sing, as did his brother Fred a year later when he was convicted of another swindle.

Still, they weren't about to turn their backs on a profession they had worked so hard to master. When they emerged from prison, they devoted themselves to business as usual, fleecing the gullible and greedy. In 1924, when Charley was sixty-five and Fred sixty, they were arrested for separating $1,300 from an out-of-towner via their patented race-wire scam. They ended up walking away scot-free. The mark had been too embarrassed to testify.

The Sunshine Boys

On the movie screen, their names are Lewis and Clark. Once they were a famous comedy team, best known for their classic "doctor sketch." Now they are crotchety old men who can't occupy the same room for five minutes without tangling in a knock-down-drag-out verbal brawl.

In real-life, they were known as Smith and Dale. One of the most successful comedy duos in the history of vaudeville, they were most often associated with their celebrated skit "Dr. Kronkheit's Only Living Patient." Their comedy was based on nonstop bickering, taken to hilariously absurd extremes.

When Neil Simon's play *The Sunshine Boys* opened on Broadway in 1972, there was no doubt that his Lewis and Clark were fictional derivatives of Smith and Dale. With the success of the play and the 1975 release of the popular film starring Walter Matthau and George Burns, renewed attention was focused on the true-life Sunshine Boys. Charlie Dale had died just a year before the appearance of Simon's play, but Joe Smith, then eighty-eight years old, went on to enjoy the new notoriety, giving interviews, lecturing at schools, and even landing a gig on the short-lived Dial-A-Joke phone line. But he was always quick to point out that there was a huge difference between the Smith and Dale team and Simon's fictional version of the comedians. Smith and Dale did, in fact, first get to know each other while locking horns in a street-corner argument, but once they became a team they were the closest of friends, a far cry from the relentlessly combative Matthau and Burns on screen. When they did disagree, it was not personal. "Oh yes, we argued," Smith once said, "but it was always about the act." In a business where partnerships rarely last a decade, these two men managed to stay together for seventy years.

The argument that brought them together occurred on the Lower East Side of New York City in 1898. Teenagers at the time, they were not yet Joe Smith and Charlie Dale. They were still using their family names of, respectively, Sultzer and Marks. Both had rented bicycles and were spending a Sunday afternoon pedaling around the neighborhood. They met when they collided. As a yelling match began over who caused the accident, the shop owner who had rented out the bikes overheard the boys and noticed something about the way they went at each other. He told them there was something funny about them, funny enough for the shop owner to pay them an enormous compliment. He said their give-and-take reminded him of Weber and Fields. In those days, Weber and Fields were the premier ethnic comics on the vaudeville stage, famous for their thick Germanic accents, their fractured English, and their finely honed banter. The shop owner encouraged Sultzer and Marks to become friends, and they decided to give it a try.

Watching a vaudeville comedy team perform one day inspired them to put their newfound friendship to work on the stage. They put together a grab-bag act that combined singing, dancing, and telling jokes, and landed their first jobs at Bowery saloons. As they acquired valuable experience, they also acquired new names. They were slated to perform at the Palace Gardens, a combination restaurant and entertainment hall, and showed up for their first night's performance to find a sign outside announcing that some other team named

Smith and Dale would be appearing there instead. Crestfallen, they were sure they had been fired for some mysterious reason. Then they got the real story from Sultzer's brother. The brother had agreed to get a set of business cards made for them, but when he showed up at the print shop, he came up with a better idea. It turned out that a team named Smith and Dale had just decided to try new stage names and had left an unpaid-for order of new cards with the old names at the print shop. The cards could be bought at a steep discount. So Sultzer and Marks became Smith and Dale thanks to a print-shop bargain.

The team's specialty soon became sketches, typically revolving around delirious doings in commonplace settings. Their Yiddish-accented skits included "The New Schoolteacher," "Hungarian Rhapsody" (set in a Hungarian restaurant), and "The False Alarm Fire Company." Their interaction was fast, precisely timed, and uproarious. Often they relied on flights of skewed logic. In a delicatessen skit, Smith played the customer and Dale portrayed the shop owner:

SMITH: Good morning.
DALE: Good afternoon.
SMITH: Good evening.
DALE: Good night—make a day of it.
SMITH: I've only got five minutes to spend a nickel. Gimme five
       cents' worth of that salmon.
DALE: That's not salmon, that's ham.
SMITH: Did I ask you what it was?

Mostly, the material seemed secondary—many of the jokes were downright corny—but their delivery could make virtually anything funny. This was never more true than in "Dr. Kronkheit's Only Living Patient." With Dale as Dr. Kronkheit ("kronk," incidentally, is Yiddish for sick) and Smith as the patient, they would trade lines with furious speed and perfectly tuned inflections. Smith would run through a catalog of nonsensical complaints ("Doctor, I'm sick. Every time I eat a heavy meal I'm not so hungry after."), while the two parried their way through nonstop bouts of wordplay:

KRONKHEIT: No, no . . . please, my time is liniment.
PATIENT: Don't rub it in.
KRONKHEIT: I have no patience!
PATIENT: I shouldn't be here either.

They first performed their doctor sketch in 1906. By that time, they had already graduated from beer halls to the big-time vaudeville circuits that sent them to theaters across the country. At the time, vaudeville's variety-show format was the great popular-entertainment medium, the television of its day. But unlike TV, vaudeville allowed comedians to fine-tune their routines as they performed the same act in one city after another. Appearing between singers, dancers, jugglers, performing monkeys, and midget acts, Smith and Dale honed their patter to a razorlike sharpness and learned to customize their sketches to suit whatever audience they faced. Their comedy act became so funny and so popular that they were invited across the Atlantic to perform throughout Great Britain, where they proved equally successful.

Even after vaudeville faded in the 1920s, Smith and Dale continued to be in demand, appearing on Broadway, in films, on radio, and eventually on television. Throughout, unlike Neil Simon's Lewis and Clark, they managed to steer clear of any major rifts between them. A major point of contention between Simon's characters was Lewis's (Burns's) habit of poking his partner in the chest and spraying as he enunciated certain letters. The closest Smith came to acknowledging a *Sunshine Boys*–like tension was this description of his work with Charlie Dale: "I never did poke Charlie hard. I'd point my finger at him and, if necessary, give him a little jab when I said, 'You're making a mountain out of a mothball,' but I never hurt him . . . And as for all that about my spitting in his face during the act when I pronounced my t's, why, it was *he* who spit in *my* face when he pronounced his p's!"

Clearly, though, the partnership was coupled with an enduring affection. Smith commissioned a tombstone to be prepared when his partner died in 1971 and he ordered that the inscription read "Smith and Dale." He was determined that they would remain a team even in death.

Sweet Smell of Success

Burt Lancaster was never more imposing than he was in this 1957 film. As the powerful Broadway columnist J. J. Hunsecker, he manipulates everyone who courts his favor with a ruthlessness so cold-blooded that it is virtually reptilian. His low-keyed, bristling intensity is remarkable, even compared with other intense Lancaster performances. Obviously, the actor's talent was a major ingredient in this outstanding characterization, but much of the credit belongs to other people as well. First among them would be the film's screenwriters, Ernest Lehman and Clifford Odets, for crafting the film's exceptionally caustic dialogue, and to Lehman once again for creating the Hunsecker character in his novella that was the basis for the film. A tip of the hat would also have to go to the one man who made the whole thing possible, Lehman's original unwitting inspiration, columnist Walter Winchell.

Baby Boomers may know Winchell solely as the ringing, staccato narrator's voice of the original *Untouchables* TV series. Their parents' generation, though, remembers him as the flamboyant newspaperman and radio commentator who almost single-handedly invented the gossip industry and established himself as the premier media icon of his day. In appearance, he differed drastically from Lancaster's Hunsecker. With his severe crew cut and grim, spectacled visage, Hunsecker is intimidation personified. In contrast, Winchell was a good-looking man with an affable smile, a man who was photogenic enough to star in several Hollywood films. As for the power that Hunsecker wields on screen, *Sweet Smell of Success* did not have to resort to fictional invention.

From the 1920s to the 1940s, Winchell reigned supreme among columnists dealing in inside scoops from the worlds of entertainment, high society, and, at his height, politics as well. *Sweet Smell* author Lehman, a New York press agent for a number of years, observed close-up the fear and desperate loyalty that Winchell provoked among publicists. Placing an item for one's client in Winchell's column was the press agent's ultimate goal, sometimes the key to a client's overnight success, translating into lucrative job offers for a performer or a sudden influx of customers for a nightclub. Landing on Winchell's so-called Drop Dead List, on the other hand, amounted to the kiss of death. To avoid this plunge into professional Siberia, press agents would go to any length to stay in Winchell's good graces. Sometimes, Winchell-toadying could reach comical extremes. One day, publicist Jack Tirman found himself among a group of fellow press agents who actually had the nerve to swap complaints about the king of columnists. Tirman grew fearful at being associated with such blasphemy. Looking heavenward, he cried, "I'm not listening, Walter!"

Although he reached the top through salacious, irreverent gossip-mongering, Winchell came from an altogether different background. He was descended from a devout Russian-Jewish family of rabbis and cantors. He began his professional life in 1910 at the age of thirteen when he joined a juvenile musical troupe on the vaudeville stage. He continued his song-and-dance career as an adult but was never more than a marginal success. Casting about for ways to supplement his income, he started a column for a vaudeville trade paper while in his twenties, and in a few years was able to parlay that experience into a job with a New York daily. His coverage of the Broadway scene intrigued readers and built a following. His ability to ferret out the most enticing tidbits about the celebrities of the day, coupled with his slangy, telegraphic writing style, made him the perfect audacious voice for the rambunctious 1920s. A decade later, after he joined the Hearst tabloid *The New York Daily Mirror*, he rose to a new plateau of influence. Now that the Great Depression had enveloped the country in a more somber mood, he became the virtual mouthpiece for the FDR administration, both in print and over the radio airwaves. A confidant of the president, he served as a media pipeline from the White House to the public, transmitting New Deal scoops available to no other journalist.

At the same time that he championed social and economic reforms, Winchell continued to keep in touch with more frivolous concerns. Even though most Americans were struggling just to put food on the table, they were still curious about those privileged few who had money to burn. Thanks to Winchell, they could still read and hear about the glamorous and risqué doings in what was called "café society," the New York subculture of exclusive nightclub life that revolved primarily around such glamorous establishments as El Morocco and the Stork Club. It was at the Stork Club that Winchell had his own perpetually reserved table, where he could observe the café-society scene up close and hold court amid all those who sought his attention. (In *Sweet Smell of Success*, this setting was switched to the 21 Club.)

After World War II, with the Depression over and fascism defeated, Winchell sought a new cause on which he could hold forth. Always eager to tap into public groundswells, he turned away from Roosevelt's New Dealism and instead embraced rabid anticommunism. His new inside-government contact was Senator Joseph McCarthy, and his column and radio show became vehicles for Red-baiting. At his most vicious, he lashed out at New York *Post* editor James Wechsler, attempting over and over again to smear him as a commie stooge.

Not all of Winchell's vendettas at the time were political. A deeply personal one concerned his daughter Walda and an unwanted suitor named Billy Cahn—unwanted by Winchell, that is. His efforts to destroy

Cahn formed the basis for the plot of *Sweet Smell of Success*. In the film, Hunsecker wants to drive a wedge between his beautiful, neurotic sister and a jazz musician. He instructs a hustling young press agent (Tony Curtis) to break up the engagement by any means necessary. Eventually, Curtis plants a packet of marijuana on the musician (Martin Milner), who is then arrested and beaten by a thuggish plainclothesman.

While the Martin Milner character was an upstanding young man, Billy Cahn, his real-life counterpart, could not quite make the same claim. He liked to refer to himself as a Broadway producer, and actually produced a couple of plays, but he devoted most of his time to gambling and shady schemes, and had served two short jail terms before meeting Winchell's daughter. Still, Cahn and Walda did seem to be genuinely in love—not that that made any difference to Walda's father. He used his column and broadcasts to brand Cahn as a dangerous criminal, even hinting at one point that he might be capable of murder. He also used his influence with New York's district attorney to have Cahn picked up for questioning. Unlike J. J. Hunsecker, he did not arrange for Cahn to be framed for drug possession, but he apparently turned to his friend J. Edgar Hoover for help. According to one source, Hoover instigated an Internal Revenue investigation that led to Cahn's conviction and eighteen-month prison sentence for tax evasion.

By the time *Sweet Smell of Success* was released, Winchell's vaunted influence was already on the wane. As Neal Gabler makes clear in his biography of the columnist, the times had passed Winchell by. In effect, the film trounced somebody who was already half-beaten. Winchell's opportunistic Red-baiting may have kept him in the public eye during the early 1950s, but his primary beats, café society and the Broadway scene, were no longer objects of fascination for the public. What's more, his radio commentary show had fallen out of favor with the introduction of television, a medium that Winchell was never able to master. Burt Lancaster's scathing characterization, of course, didn't help matters. By the time Winchell started narrating the Prohibition-era exploits of *The Untouchables* in 1960, he was already an anachronism, attaching himself to a program that dramatized bygone days.

Over the course of his long career, Winchell learned many tricks of the media-celebrity game. One thing he never learned was how to quit while he was ahead. In the remaining twelve years of his life following the debut of *The Untouchables,* he repeatedly tried to recapture his fame and power, without success.

To Die For

Though it's classified as a comedy, Gus Van Sant's *To Die For* isn't exactly full of yuks. A scathing satire on America's obsession with celebrity (no matter how sleazily achieved), it's a deeply unsettling film, ultimately far more chilling than funny. It's no surprise that its director went on to shoot a controversial remake of *Psycho*.

Indeed, Suzanne Stone—the lethally ditsy main character, played to perfection by the mouthwatering Nicole Kidman—is every bit as sociopathic as Norman Bates. Beneath her cheerleader exterior, she is a frighteningly ruthless femme fatale, whose single-minded ambition is to make it big in the media. The credo she lives by is repeated throughout the film: "You aren't really anybody in America if you're not on TV. Because what's the point of doing anything worthwhile if nobody's watching?"

Inconveniently, she happens to be wed to Larry Maretto, an easygoing lug (engagingly played by Matt Dillon) whose old-fashioned family values are in conflict with Suzanne's hard-driving, completely egotistical dreams. When Larry puts his foot down and refuses to move to L.A., his wife has no other choice than to arrange for his cold-blooded murder. Employing her considerable sexual charms, she seduces a love-struck high-school loser named Jimmy Emmett (a creepily effective Joaquin Phoenix) and enlists him and a pal to do the job. The crime rockets Suzanne onto the front page of every tabloid in the country, providing her (however briefly) with the kind of media celebrity she's always coveted. The story ends on a deeply gratifying note, as Suzanne gets her just deserts at the hands of a "Hollywood producer" (played by horror director David Cronenberg) who is really a Mafia hitman.

The film (with a wickedly clever script by Buck Henry, who puts in an appearance as a sour-tempered high-school teacher) was based on a novel by Joyce Maynard (who can also be seen in a cameo as Suzanne's lawyer). Its ultimate source, however, was the true-life case of twenty-two-year-old Pamela Smart (*née* Wojas). Smart wasn't an insanely ambitious cable-TV weathergirl. Nor did she end up getting whacked by a suave mafiosi. But in most other respects, *To Die For* sticks close to the facts of her sensational story.

Born in Miami, Pam moved to New Hampshire at an early age when her parents decided that the crime-ridden city was no place to raise their little girl. Full of warm memories of her native state, she returned to Florida for college. While visiting her parents in New Hampshire during spring break, she met and fell love in with a handsome young insurance salesman named Greg Smart. Two years later, they were married.

Pam went to work at a local high school as the director of the media center. To all outward appearances, she and Greg seemed like perfectly contented newlyweds. In reality, their marriage was troubled from the start. Just seven months after they tied the knot, Greg confessed that he'd already had a fling with another woman.

At the time, Pam was running the high school's Drug and Alcohol Awareness program. One of her student counselors was a shy, slender, fifteen-year-old named Billy Flynn. Before long, Billy found himself the object of Pam's increasingly overheated attentions. She began sending him cheesecake snapshots of herself in skimpy bikinis. One weekend in February, while her husband was away on a trip, she invited Billy to stay overnight in her condomium. They drank liquor while watching the cheesy S/M movie *9 1/2 Weeks*. Later that night, they became lovers.

It's easy to imagine that the fifteen-year-old boy—who'd never had sex before—must have felt as if he'd died and gone to XXX-rated heaven. In any case, he quickly found himself in thrall to the older, far more experienced woman. Just as in the movie, she began telling her teen lover that her husband was a violently abusive beast. She couldn't divorce him, however, without losing everything—her furniture, the condo, even her beloved little dog. The only possible solution was disposing of Greg.

At first, Billy shrugged off the suggestion. Pam, however, became increasingly insistent—and threatening. In effect, she began sexually blackmailing the boy. If he wanted to keep their relationship going, he would have to kill Greg. Otherwise, she would find someone else— someone more worthy of her favors—to do the job.

With the inducement of $500 apiece (to be procured from Greg's life insurance policy), Billy enlisted the help of two high-school pals, Patrick "Pete" Randall and Vance "J. R." Lattime. On the night of May 1, 1990—while Pam was busily (and conveniently) engaged elsewhere— Billy and Pete entered the Smarts' condo through the back door, which had been left unlocked by prearrangement. After ransacking the place to make it look as if it had been burglarized, they waited for Greg to get home. As soon as he stepped through the door, the two boys grabbed him, forced him to his knees, and held a butcher knife to his throat. While the twenty-four-year-old man pleaded for his life, Billy pulled out a .38 revolver and shot him once through the head. The two teen assassins then fled from the condo and escaped in a getaway car driven by J. R. Lattime.

In the days following the murder, rumors abounded. Greg, some people said, had been bumped off because of gambling debts he'd run up in Atlantic City. Others claimed that the Hell's Angels were involved. In the meantime, Pam seemed suspiciously lighthearted for a young, devoted widow whose spouse had just been savagely murdered in the front hallway of their home. She seemed to revel in all the media attention being lavished on her, and couldn't wait to clear the condo of her late husband's possessions.

Greg's devastated parents (especially his father, with whom Greg had been especially close) became increasingly suspicious of Pam. So

did investigators. Within a very short time, those suspicions were confirmed by an anonymous call to the local police, tipping them off to
Pam's involvement with Billy Flynn. On June 12, 1990, the three boys
were arrested and, soon afterward, certified to stand trial as adults.
Faced with the prospect of life imprisonment, Billy broke down and
confessed.

At first, Pam professed absolute shock and disbelief at Billy's confession. Indeed, she claimed that they'd never been lovers. Under pressure
from police, however, another high-schooler—a chunky girl named
Cecilia Piece, who had been Pam's student aide and confidant—verified
Billy's account, insisting that she'd once walked in on the mismatched
lovebirds while they were having sex. Allowing herself to be wired,
Cecilia recorded a highly incriminating conversation with Pam in
which the pretty, perky, oh-so-innocent young woman spewed out an
ugly, profanity-ridden diatribe that amounted to a full confession.

Brought to trial in March 1991, Pam continued to claim that—while
she might have made an error in allowing her feelings for Billy to get
out of hand—she had nothing to do with the murder. The romantically
obsessed Billy, she insisted, had committed it entirely of his own
accord, driven by sexual jealousy. In the end, however, the jury found
Billy's tearful, lurid tale of sexual manipulation at the hands of the
scheming older woman far more convincing. On March 22, 1991, Pam
Smart was found guilty of being an accomplice to first-degree murder,
conspiracy to commit murder, and witness tampering. She was sentenced to life imprisonment without the possibility of parole. Billy
Flynn, who had cut a deal with the state, received a reduced sentence
of twenty-eight years to life.

The Warriors

Based on Sol Yurick's 1965 novel, Walter Hill's *The Warriors* gained instant notoriety at the time of its release in 1979. Promoted as an ultraviolent exploitation film, it sparked a rash of shootings and gang fights in inner-city theaters, whose audiences apparently identified a little too closely with the film's combative characters. These incidents provoked the predictable outcries from tongue-clucking critics, who denounced the film as a piece of mindless, violence-mongering Hollywood trash. Other critics, however, came to its defense, most notably Pauline Kael, influential reviewer for *The New Yorker* magazine, who praised the film as "a real moviemaker's movie . . . mesmerizing in its intensity."

The plot has a classic simplicity. The nine, multiracial members of the title gang (whose colors consist of brown leather vests worn over bare torsos) leave their home turf in Coney Island and travel to the darkest Bronx to attend a convocation of New York's leading street gangs. The meeting has been called by a charismatic leader named Cyrus, a true (if sociopathic) visionary who plans to unite the boroughs' sixty thousand gang members into one giant army and take over the city (which has a police force of only twenty thousand). Everyone applauds this scheme, except for the leader of the Rogues, a wild-eyed psycho who guns down Cyrus, then frames the Warriors for the assassination. The rest of the film follows the Warriors as they try to make their way back to Brooklyn, a trip that requires them to run a gauntlet of rival gangs out for their blood—the pin-striped Baseball Furies, the outcast Orphans, the lesbian Lizzies, and others.

With its rock-and-roll soundtrack, kung fu choreography, surreal urban nightscape, and futuristic *Clockwork Orange* costumes, *The Warriors* seems like the kind of hip, stylized action-fantasy that only Hollywood could dream up. So it comes as a surprise to learn that it is rooted in ancient history—that it is actually an updated, fictionalized telling of something that happened in 401 B.C. and that was recorded by a Greek historian and writer named Xenophon in his book *Anabasis*.

Anabasis (a word that can be roughly translated as the "Up-Country March") chronicles the ill-fated military expedition undertaken by Cyrus the Younger, brother of Artaxerxes II, king of the Persian Empire. In 401 B.C., the charismatic Cyrus resolved to dethrone his older brother and assume the kingship himself. Assembling a force that included ten thousand Greek mercenaries, he led his soldiers from Sardis to the gates of Babylon, where they were met by the army of the king. A ferocious battle ensued, during which Cyrus was slain. Shortly afterward, under the pretext of negotiating an armistice, a treacherous Persian leader invited the surviving Greek generals to a meeting, where they were immediately seized and put to death.

The remaining Greek mercenaries now found themselves in dire circumstances—leaderless, alone in unknown territory, with enemy troops and hostile tribes surrounding them, and more than a thousand miles separating them from home. It was at this point that Xenophon took charge. A master tactician (as well as a brilliant writer-philosopher who was close friends with Socrates), the thirty-year-old Xenophon rallied his comrades and proposed that they retreat northward up the Tigris River. After electing him leader, the Greeks embarked on this perilous journey.

Along the way, they were compelled not only to negotiate an alien, often inimical landscape but to do battle with a host of enemies, from the pursuing forces of the Persian king to the savage mountain tribes of Kurdistan. These episodes are captured in vivid detail in Xenophon's account (written from his personal notes not long after his return).

At one point, for example, a large force of Persians—led by a general named Mithradates—attacked the Greeks, who were unable to retaliate because their own bows had a much shorter range than the Persian models. Following this battle—during which the Greek rearguard suffered severe losses—Xenophon organized a troop of Rhodian slingers, whose weapons not only employed lead bullets (instead of stones) but had twice the range of anything in the Persian arsenal. During their next encounter, the Greeks turned the tables, inflicting heavy casualties on the enemy. Afterward, as Xenophon wrote, "the Greek troops, unbidden save by their own impulse, disfigured the bodies of the dead, in order that the sight of them might inspire the utmost terror in the enemy."

Five months after they first set off on their retreat, the bulk of the Greek forces arrived safely on the shores of the Euxine River—a spectacular feat of military survival that became legendary as the march of "The Ten Thousand" (and would eventually serve as the inspiration for the peril-filled odyssey portrayed in *The Warriors*). Today, Xenophon's *Anabasis* is regarded not only as a gripping, gracefully written adventure but as a major contribution to the science of warfare. "After the lapse of twenty-three centuries," one modern historian has written, "there is no better military textbook than the *Anabasis*."

The Wild Geese

"I should have taken Richard Burton and Roger Moore along with me and we'd have had a happy ending."

—Mad Mike Hoare, the inspiration for the hero of *The Wild Geese,* commenting on a mercenary operation not nearly as successful as the one portrayed on film

In **real life**, mercenaries have gotten their share of bad press. In movies, they generally come off a lot better. High-minded observers of the international scene might characterize them as amoral killers for hire, but action-movie fans tend to see them merely as modern-day adventurers, a bit rough around the edges perhaps, but still the sort of antiheroes that can deliver high-powered excitement, whether it comes packaged in prestige productions (*The Dogs of War*), low-budget potboilers (*Mercenary Fighters*), or glib Schwarzenegger romps (*Commando*).

One of the most popular of the soldier-of-fortune adventures, and certainly one of the most realistic, is *The Wild Geese.* Starring Richard Burton, Richard Harris, and Roger Moore, this 1978 film provides a detailed depiction of a British mercenary mission to rescue an imprisoned African leader. Some of the credit for the movie's realism goes to its technical adviser, Colonel Mike Hoare. Few other men could have brought his sort of knowledge to the project. Hoare was a notorious mercenary himself, whose exploits in Africa during the 1960s were legendary—or deplorable, depending on your point of view. The makers of *The Wild Geese* relied on him in more ways than one. They drew upon his expertise and also made use of him as a template for the central character played by Richard Burton.

Burton's character, named Colonel Faulkner, is recruited out of retirement to mastermind the intricate, dangerous mission. He is clearly regarded as the foremost mercenary leader of his day, although his past exploits are only vaguely defined. At the time *The Wild Geese* was filmed, Colonel Hoare had also been retired from mercenary work for many years. The exploits that accounted for his reputation had occurred fourteen years earlier, in 1964, when he had commanded a unit of hired soldiers in the civil-war-torn Congo. Officially the unit was called Five Commando. Their unofficial moniker was the Wild Geese, a tribute by the Irish Hoare to renegade Irish-Catholic soldiers who left their homeland behind after the Protestant takeover of the island in 1691.

In the Richard Burton film, it is clear that Colonel Faulkner's paramilitary escapades have often been regarded as unsavory. In real life, Colonel Hoare has also come in for some criticism. But controversial as he has been, there is one thing most people can agree upon.

Hoare ranks as one of the most daring military adventurers ever to emerge from the accountancy profession.

Incongruously enough, the figuring of assets, liabilities, and profits was the vocation Mike Hoare followed after World War II. As chronicled in Anthony Mockler's *The New Mercenaries*, Hoare had served with the British army in the Far East during the war, but the exact nature of his service is not clear. When the war ended, he emigrated from Ireland to South Africa. There he plied his pencil-pushing trade, acquired a family complete with five kids, invested money in a used-car dealership, and became an official in his local yachting club. Hardly, it would seem, the makings of a blood-and-guts soldier for hire. But under the surface of his Rotarian lifestyle there was simmering a desire for something more audacious. In his spare time he dabbled in documentary filmmaking and went on nonleisurely cruises in a wooden dinghy, one of which ended in a boat wreck in shark-infested waters. To satisfy his adventure lust, he also organized and led tourist safaris. One of these took him to the Congolese province of Katanga. The knowledge he gained of the area would lead to a serious change in life for Hoare.

In 1960, Katanga attempted to break away from the newly independent Congo. Hoare did not join the mercenary forces recruited to fight in that conflict, but he was hired by a South African tycoon to find the man's son, reported missing in the area. Leading a small, armed search party, Hoare discovered that the young man had been murdered in accordance with a brutal tribal ritual. Finding that he could not bring the millionaire's son back alive, he did what he considered the next best thing: he destroyed the village where the killing took place.

The severe efficiency of Hoare's actions made an impression on certain officials in the area. He also developed contacts with the right people through another South African used-car dealer who had turned to the soldier-of-fortune business. When civil war broke out once more in the Congo in 1964, the forty-five-year-old Hoare was hired to lead a mercenary commando force.

Katanga had been reunited with the rest of the burgeoning nation, but now the Simba tribe was rebelling against the central government. The Simbas were taking hostages by the hundreds and killing foreigners and spreading terror throughout the area. To fight them on behalf of Premier Moise Tshombe, Hoare assembled Five Commando from the growing number of white mercenaries who were converging on Africa at the time. Some of them were recruited through newspaper ads that sought "fit young men looking for employment with a difference."

In a sixteen-month period, Hoare's Wild Geese helped defeat the Simba rebellion through lightning-strike tactics. Fashioning his troops as a sort of motorized cavalry, Hoare sent his men driving high speed in armored Jeeps through enemy-held towns with mounted machine guns blazing. As they rolled quickly across the country, the Wild Geese rescued many missionaries and nuns who had been either menaced or held hostage by the Simbas. Although these people obviously approved of the Wild Geese operations, many politicians and news commentators denounced Hoare, or "Mad Mike," as they called him. For them, the very idea of soldiers killing for the highest bidder was contemptible.

Hoare's Congo contract resulted in great military success, but for years it did not lead to any other mercenary assignments. Although an offer would periodically come his way, nothing panned out. Instead he lived off money made from his Congo employers and from the rights to his story that he sold to newspapers. By the time he was advising the production of *The Wild Geese* in 1978, though, he was anxious to take another military fling. And he had a particular operation in mind.

A coup had taken place in the Seychelles islands off Africa's east coast. Hoare sold the deposed president on his plan to reinstate the leader. A mercenary team of about fifty men would arrive in the Seychelles airport, posing as a group of three traveling rugby teams. Each man would carry a cricket bag fitted with a false bottom. Concealed in each bag would be an AK-47 automatic rifle. Once in place on the island, Hoare believed, they could carry out a swift, relatively bloodless countercoup.

On November 25, 1981, Hoare and his men stepped off their plane in the Seychelles, and they all succeeded in passing through customs with their hidden weapons—all except one. From there the whole operation quickly unraveled.

After a skirmish with government troops at the airport, the mercenaries seized upon a way out of the situation. Like the actor-mercenaries in the final scenes of *The Wild Geese*, they commandeered a plane and made a hairbreadth escape. They directed the plane to the safety of Louis Botha Airport in Durban, South Africa. Or at least they seemed to have reached safety, but then daring escapes in real life can lead to the sort of complications that fictional adventurers need not worry about. As it turned out, South African authorities were compelled by international pressure to arrest the mercenaries on the charge of hijacking.

They convicted all of them. Most of the group received light punishment, but Hoare, serving as an example for others, was sentenced to ten years. He was released after four.

Summing up the Seychelles fiasco, Hoare said, "I should have taken Richard Burton and Roger Moore along with me and we'd have had a happy ending."

The Wild One

He comes barreling down the open road, astraddle his growling motorcycle, an aviator's cap perched rakishly on his head, dark sunglasses concealing his eyes, a sneer playing on his lips. Over forty years ago, this image of Marlon Brando as *The Wild One* came to symbolize free-spirited, engine-gunning rebellion, the pinnacle of fifties cool. *Or*—depending on your point of view—it came to represent the disintegration of civility and order, the onset of a new barbarism. This 1954 film, the first of the outlaw-biker flicks and a benchmark in postwar pop culture, attracted a youthful following, but at the same time triggered a sense of outrage. In England, the movie was so controversial that it was banned for fourteen years. In a similar way, opinions have split over the real incident that spawned this seminal counterculture film. When motorcycle clubs converged on the small California town of Hollister in 1947, did they simply cut loose for some good-natured, rowdy fun? Or did they run amok and seize the town in a grip of terror, as some headlines claimed at the time?

The Wild One first began to take shape early in 1951 when producer Stanley Kramer noticed a short story in *Harper's* magazine entitled "The Cyclists' Raid." The piece provided a fictionalized version of the

Hollister incident and would become the official source material for the Brando movie, even though it bore little resemblance to what was eventually rendered on screen. The one key element that was used in the film was the climactic accidental killing, when one of the towns-people is run over by a motorcycle (the victim in the story is a young woman; in the film the victim is an old man). In the *Harper's* story, unlike Kramer's movie, the motorcycle gang is a regimented, almost paramilitary group of young men who go wild once they get a few beers under their belts. The film's portrait of the cyclists as scruffy noncon-formists was closer to the truth.

The biker phenomenon that led to the real *Wild One* story was fueled by restless veterans returning home to California after World War II. Not ready to settle down completely into a domesticated life, they formed motorcycle clubs for weekend jaunts of drinking, woman-izing, and hard riding. The notorious Hell's Angels began this way, along with many other lesser known groups. The Independence Day week-end of 1947 would bring the phenomenon to national attention.

On Friday night, July 4, various motorcycle clubs rolled into Hollis-ter—some ninety miles south of San Francisco—for a nearby racing and hill-climb event. Approximately 750 cycles rumbled into town that weekend while many other biker enthusiasts arrived by car. Among the clubs that showed up were the Nomads, the Booze Fighters, and the P.O.B.O.B.'s, whose full name—the Pissed Off Bastards of Blooming-ton—might have served as a clue that there was a possibility of trouble. In all, four thousand visitors came to Hollister, nearly doubling the pop-ulation of the town.

Once the bikers got drunk, they hit upon the idea of staging their own impromptu races and started tearing down the main thoroughfare in town. From there, as beer continued to flow, the celebrating esca-lated and didn't wind down for another thirty-six hours. The bikers pissed in the street, chucked beer cans through shop windows, and rode their cycles through restaurants and hotel lobbies. Brawls flared up here and there, but to the bikers' credit, they kept the fisticuffs to themselves. Unlike the sort of mayhem portrayed in later biker flicks of the sixties, they didn't prey upon local women or brutalize any of the men in town. And unlike both the *Harper's* story and the Brando film, nobody died from a fatal motorcycle accident.

Some townspeople, particularly some of the shop owners, were not at all incensed by the hell-raising episode. Not only did the motorcyclists patronize their establishments, but business would flourish even more in weeks to come when curiosity seekers arrived in town to get a look at the site of the much-reported spree. (This mercenary attitude translated into one of the film's themes, as Kramer and company dramatized the town's hypocritical handling of the situation.) The most disturbing aspect of the weekend binge was the local police's complete inability to enforce the law. Hollister's constabulary consisted of only seven men, and they clearly were not accustomed to controlling such a tumultuous situation. Eventually, Hollister officials were able to restore order only when they called in thirty-two officers from neighboring counties. The special combined force pulled in thirty-eight bikers, who were then sentenced to various minor charges in a special session of the local police court.

During the filming of *The Wild One*, the line between real and reel was blurred to a certain extent. In order to prepare for his role, Brando rode with bikers involved in the Hollister rally and apparently was accepted as part of the club. And some of these bikers, in turn, were featured in the movie as motorcycle gang members. One of them ended up supplying the movie's most memorable line. Kramer asked the biker one day what he was rebelling against. "Well, what ya got?" the biker replied, an answer that Brando eventually paraphrased on film.

Although Brando emerged from this movie as a hipster icon, some viewers believed that the most convincing biker in the film was supporting actor Lee Marvin. Like many motorcycle club members in those days, he was a World War II veteran, and a decorated one at that, and a genuine badass in his own right. Sonny Barger, the future head of the Hell's Angels, who was fourteen at the time the movie came out, said that Marvin was his idol and "definitely the hero of the movie." Later he would buy the jersey worn by Marvin in the film.

Any indignation experienced by the citizens of Hollister in 1947 seemed to have faded by 1997 when the town staged a fiftieth-anniversary celebration of the notorious "wild one" weekend. Thousands of bikers arrived in town—invited this time—to take in the July 4 fireworks and browse through 150 concession booths selling food and souvenirs. Once perceived as a deplorable invasion, the 1947 incident was overtaken by nostalgia and a sense of acceptance. According to a 1997 Hollister city councilman, who had been only a boy at the time of the original escapade, the 1947 biker orgy "wasn't that bad. There were just too many of them, and it got out of hand."

Index

Harold Schechter and **David Everitt** have written several books together, including *The Manly Movie Guide*. On his own, Schechter is the author of a bestselling series of true crime books.